Becoming Human

MERCER
UNIVERSITY PRESS

Endowed by

TOM WATSON BROWN

and

THE WATSON-BROWN FOUNDATION, INC.

BECOMING HUMAN

KIERKEGAARDIAN REFLECTIONS ON ETHICAL MODELS IN LITERATURE

JAMIE LORENTZEN

MERCER UNIVERSITY PRESS MACON, GEORGIA

MUP/ P515

Published by Mercer University Press
1400 Coleman Avenue
Macon, Georgia 31207

9 8 7 6 5 4 3 2 1

Books published by Mercer University Press are printed on acid-free paper that meets the requirements of the American National Standard for Information Sciences—Permanence of Paper for Printed Library Materials.

ISBN 978-0-88146-541-9
Cataloging-in-Publication Data is available from the Library of Congress

Contents

To Jane,

for reading and walking

together through life

Notes and Acknowledgements

Chapters are derived from four lecture series presented between 2004 and 2013 at United Lutheran Church, Red Wing, Minnesota. The Coda is a tribute to the late Professor Howard V. Hong (St. Olaf College), without whom the following text would not have been composed.

The frontispiece is from Chapter 31 of the first edition of Mark Twain's *Adventures of Huckleberry Finn* (New York: Charles L. Webster and Company, 1885).

Page numbers in parentheses following citations from Søren Kierkegaard texts correspond to *Søren Kierkegaards Samlede Værker*.

Many thanks to the Friends of the Howard V. & Edna H. Hong Kierkegaard Library, the Kierkegaard House Foundation, and Friends and House Foundation member Andy Burgess for generously supporting this publication.

Finally, just as Huck Finn sometimes thought until he wore his head sore, my dear wife Jane thought until she wore her head sore about my sometimes unruly syntax in the manuscript of this book. Thanks, Jane, for your invaluable critical advice and generous heart. And… sorry about the sore head….

Introduction

One important question underlying the intent of this book—*Why read good books well?*—is not new. American humorist Mark Twain (1835-1910) hints at it more than a century ago when he noted how a classic is a book people praise but don't read.[1] Another fifty years before him, Danish author Søren Kierkegaard (1813-55) also writes about the subject humorously: "Who in our day thinks of wasting any time on the curious idea that it is an art to be a good reader, not to mention spending time to become that?"[2]

Perhaps reading is merely meant to offer a reader some immediate esthetic pleasure or sense of temporary escape or distraction from an increasingly distracting, distracted world. Perhaps reading is a simple act that exists for its own sake, just as some art is made for the sake of the art itself. But if it is an art to be a good reader, something seems lacking if a reader reads exclusively for the above reasons—something that has to do with the reader's capacity to reflect upon issues related to the book—for, as Kierkegaard also notes: "anyone who reads a book for one or another superficial reason unrelated to the book is not a genuine reader."[3]

The art of being a good reader, then, may be said to include the reader reading reflectively, which is to say reading

---

[1] Mark Twain, *Tales, Speeches, Essays, and Sketches* (New York: Penguin, 1994) 202 (from *Pudd'nhead Wilson's New Calendar*).

[2] Søren Kierkegaard, *Fear and Trembling* and *Repetition*, eds. and trs. Howard V. Hong and Edna H. Hong (Princeton: Princeton University Press, 1983), 225 (III 259, fr. *Repetition*).

[3] *Repetition*, 225 (III 259).

with a few fundamental questions in mind, like *what is the author saying? Is the author saying it well? Is it worth saying?* A reader may first do well, then, to imagine the author saying to the reader, "I have something important to say to you, but I prefer to show and not tell, for showing will make a truer impression on you because you thereby will discover meaning on your own. And so I will try to weave meaning into my book's plot, characters, and themes. If the book is good, may it be good because you not only take pleasure in my telling of the tale but also because it evokes value to your own life, something that perhaps might help you learn better to cope with and more confidently navigate the complex world in which you find yourself."

In this context, good books may be said to be written in an effort to help a reader recall, reclaim, or redeem intimations of possibility and goodness that may have been lost or forgotten by the reader somewhere along the way. They also serve to teach the reader that which the reader does not yet know or fully understand, for understanding may be considered the first step in becoming more fully human. Reading good books well, in other words, is meant to charge the reader ethically, to help the reader become more fully human by engaging the reader to live a fuller, deeper, more meaningful life—which is what Kierkegaard (one of the more assiduous authors of books on ethics) may have had in mind when he wrote about his own books: "I regard myself as a *reader* of the books, not as the author."[4]

---

[4] Søren Kierkegaard, *The Point of View: On My Work as an Author*, eds. and trs. Howard V. Hong and Edna H. Hong (Princeton: Princeton University Press, 1998) 12 (XIII 501).

Authors whose books are the focus of the following chapters—Mark Twain, Herman Melville, Henrik Ibsen, and Fyodor Dostoevsky—have something more in common than having written good books about becoming human. They also are skeptical and critical of conventions, dogma, and orthodoxy of certain offices of religious institutions—offices that, according to all of them and also to Kierkegaard, tend to mediate, dilute, cheapen, or falsify ethics rooted primarily in Judeo-Christian tradition. Their skepticism and criticism gain credence when readers recognize that all of the authors have a deep knowledge of and abiding respect for ethics rooted in religion—ethics that not only express a culture's overall secular customs and group morality but presuppose what Kierkegaard scholar Gregor Malantschuk calls "a consciousness of eternally obligatory norms, which to Kierkegaard is characteristic of the genuinely ethical." In addition, "the ethics of 'the law' in Judaism [or] commandments received from an eternal transcendent power" completed the groundwork for what Kierkegaard calls Christian ethics, or an ethic that presupposes sin and grace.[5] —Such ethics positively inform the central plots, characters, and themes of *Huckleberry Finn*, *Moby-Dick*, *Peer Gynt*, and *The Brothers Karamazov*.

Regarding "Kierkegaardian Reflections" promised by the book's title: I borrow the phrase from the title of an essay by a St. Olaf College professor who taught me and many others how to read Kierkegaard, and also how to be closely attentive to and strive to appropriate the ethical that is found in good books. ("*Ethics* is the watchword," Dr. Howard V. Hong often emphasized.) His essay is entitled, "The Comic, Satire, Irony,

---

[5] *Søren Kierkegaard's Journals and Papers*, 7 vols., eds. and trs. Howard V. and Edna H. Hong (Bloomington: Indiana University Press, 1967-1978) 1:530.

and Humor: Kierkegaardian Reflections,"[6] and although Dr. Hong only begins and ends it with direct references to Kierkegaard, his own appropriation of Kierkegaard's thought is *reflected* throughout the essay. His essay, in other words, is not intended to be a sustained, direct Kierkegaardian analysis of the comic but instead a discussion of the comic run through the lens of one who has been influenced by Kierkegaard's thought for many years. Similarly, the present book is not intended to be a sustained, direct Kierkegaardian analysis of ethical models found in a handful of good books, but rather a discussion of ethics as portrayed in several pieces of literature and run through the lens of one who has been influenced by Kierkegaard's thought for many years.

Readers familiar with Kierkegaard may see his thought reflected in more pages than those on which Kierkegaard's words are directly cited. For readers unfamiliar with Kierkegaard's works: may the following chapters serve as a less orthodox and more indirect introduction to some patterns of Kierkegaard's thought than you might find elsewhere.

•

One final note about how reading good literature well influences a reader to think and act his or her way into becoming more fully human: In his autobiography *Black Boy*, American writer Richard Wright (1908-60) is severely chided by his grandmother for reading fiction, which is something she considers to be nothing but a pack of lies and "Devil stuff." But as Richard listens to fiction being read to him as a child and as he then begins to pick up and read fiction on his own, a different reality wells up, as he notes, "from somewhere within"

[6] Howard V. Hong, "The Comic, Satire, Irony, and Humor: Kierkegaardian Reflections," *Midwest Studies in Philosophy* 1 (U.S.: Blackwell Publishing, 1976) 98-105.

him. Fiction, according to Wright, "made the world around me be, throb, live.... Reality changed, the look of things altered.... My sense of life deepened and the feel of things was different."[7] Here, Wright was becoming more fully human by reading highly charged, concentrated, imaginative, personal, subjective distillations of actuality and historical reality that are best achieved through the kind of indirect communication that great fiction offers.

Of such indirect communication—the kind that Wright's grandmother somewhat rightly calls "lies" yet somewhat wrongly demonizes, Kierkegaard writes that "all *true* communication of truth must always begin with an untruth. This is partly because it is impossible to tell the whole truth in one minute or an even shorter time. On the contrary, it takes a long, long time for that."[8] Elsewhere, Kierkegaard speaks of *deceiving* readers into certain ethical truths—all for the sake of plopping humans down into the actual world a bit more wise and more prepared to act wisely than they were before they had the opportunity to suspend their disbelief to hear or read a story. The reader "grasps the truth in imagination—it looks so inviting, he cannot escape it, he goes along—and now he stands right in the middle of actuality, and the matter is altogether different"[9]—meaning that, after truth is grasped imaginatively through fiction, the reader now has been endowed with both the gift of new knowledge and the ethical task of determining how that knowledge is to impact him or her.

---

[7] Richard Wright, *Black Boy* (New York: HarperPerennial, 1993) 45.

[8] Søren Kierkegaard, *The Book on Adler*, eds. and trs. Howard V. Hong and Edna H. Hong (Princeton: Princeton University Press, 1998), 170n. (IX B 2:3b 298-99).

[9] *Journals and Papers* 4:9 (X^4 A 264, n.d. 1851).

Put another way, personal and ethical revelations of a person's existence and actions filter through the human imagination, petitioning for meaning in a world deluged by apparent meaninglessness. When readers see themselves imaginatively in the mirror of fiction, the judgments and sympathies readers bestow upon certain fictional plots, characters, and themes may then be transferred onto readers' lives. This transfer makes matters "altogether different" because meaning in readers' lives may be revealed if each reader takes seriously how fiction is capable of informing his or her life. "There are probably words addressed to our condition exactly," Henry David Thoreau writes, "which, if we could really hear and understand, would be more salutary than the morning or the spring to our lives, and possibly put a new aspect on the face of things for us."[10]

This defense of fiction ultimately suggests that readers can learn much about the truth of their own lives by reading good books well. Humans are seldom moved when, for instance, mere facts of a birth, life, and death are stated, as on a news broadcast. We are moved when we creatively, patiently imagine the sufferings and strivings of the likes of a Huckleberry Finn through a fictional narrative that constructs the drama as only narrative can: creatively, cumulatively, imaginatively, and with patience. In such instances, Kierkegaard's assertion about how "it is impossible to tell the whole truth in one minute" gains currency.

The art of being a good reader, then, may ultimately be determined by two factors, or perhaps even only one: The first is *finding time to read* truth through fiction, which, in an

[10] Henry David Thoreau, *Walden and other Writings*, ed. Joseph Wood Krutch (New York: Bantam Books, 1981) 185 (fr. "Reading" in *Walden*).

increasingly time-addled, busy, distracted, distracting world, may be considered by some to be a dearly paid commodity. The second factor is *willing to have truths made clear*, especially when a reader knows that gaining new understanding in turn may make challenging ethical claims upon the reader that may change and thereby deepen the reader's life. Here is where each person must be allowed to judge and choose for him- or herself. That said, "What an individual is capable of may be measured by how far his *understanding* is from his *willing*," Kierkegaard writes. "What a person can understand he must also be able to make himself will. Between understanding and willing lie the excuses and evasions."[11]

If, as a writer Susan Sontag (1933-2004) notes, "literature remains one of our principle modes of understanding,"[12] and if there is a will to have truths made clear, then finding the time to read truth through fiction becomes less and less a factor because excuses and evasions become less and less credible. This is the first—and perhaps the trickiest—step in the art of reading good books well, and also of reading one's life and the world well. It becomes less tricky after that.

---

[11] *Kierkegaard's Journals and Notebooks*, vol. 2, vol. ed. George Pattison (Princeton: Princeton University Press, 2008) 275.

[12] Susan Sontag, *At the Same Time: Essays and Speeches* New York: Farrar, Strauss, and Giroux, 2007) 212.

1

The Ethicist in Mark Twain's *The Adventures of Huckleberry Finn*[1]

One: The moral landscape of Huck's hell

What does it mean to be, to become a human being? And how does a religiously charged culture positively or negatively inform such being and becoming?

These questions are relevant in Mark Twain's *Adventures of Huckleberry Finn* for at least two reasons. First: the novel, set in the 1830s, depicts a conventional brand of pre-Civil War Southern morality that was co-opted and then corrupted by a pro-slavery culture. Second: the two questions above are fundamentally evoked by a word—the n-word—which Mark Twain uses more than 200 times in his novel. American author William Styron considers the word "the most powerful secular blasphemy" in American language usage.[2] Whole books have been written on its history and linguistic development in American culture. It has inspired many American school districts and libraries since the book's 1884

---

[1] Mark Twain, *Adventures of Huckleberry Finn*, as published in *The Annotated Huckleberry Finn*, ed. Michael Patrick Hearn (New York: W. W. Norton, 2001). Chapter numbers will be cited following quoted passages.

[2] William Styron, "Huck, Continued" (*The New Yorker*, 25 June 1995) 132.

publication to ban the book. An edition came out as recently as 2011 that purged the text of the word completely.

Every primary character in the novel, black or white, speaks it. It was also very much a part of the secular and religious cultures of the 1830s South—and to lesser degrees in the North—that Mark Twain wanted to depict. Mark Twain, however, saw it as a word that designated African-Americans as property and less than human, which compels readers to confront both the pain and the injustice that the word's utterance invokes. If the n-word is silenced or denied or ignored, the injustice from which it originates and the pain that it continues to inflict may remain repressed and thereby continue to bolster a bigoted ignorance. Subsequently, his frequent use of the n-word reflects how Mark Twain's depiction of how pro-slavery morality justified itself by normalizing the word.

What I mean by *normalization* of the n-word is perhaps best clarified by a few questions I ask first-time readers of the book: *When you were reading* Huck Finn, *were you at first pained by the word, then perhaps shocked by how often the word was used? Then, as you continued to reread the word, did you just get used to it? In other words, did your resistance to the word begin to wear down whereby you might even have found yourself having become tolerant of the word, at least in the context of a pro-slavery culture?*

If readers more times than not answer "yes" to these questions, then Mark Twain was successful in compelling them to confront, through the mere repetition of the n-word, how easy it is to become anesthetized to the pain and injustice that the word symbolizes. Subsequently, when the n-word through its simple repetition becomes an accepted and sanctioned part of the culture, readers unwittingly and quietly begin to deny or repress the pain and injustice that the word represents. Readers become, in effect, dehumanized slaves to the language of a culture where some humans are not treated as genuinely human and where self-proclaimed Christians are anything but genuinely striving Christians. They become part of a culture in which the human and religious possibilities of slaves' humanity are denied while the human and religious abuses of pro-slavery individuals and cultures are dismissed. It's no wonder why the clear, wondering, wandering spirit of Huck Finn finds almost everything about his culture hard to fit into and stiff, like the starched clothes the Widow Douglas tries to make him wear. Even Huck's unwitting misspelling of the word *civilized*—with an *s* instead of a *c* (*s*ivilized)—seems an intuitive act of defiance against a corrupt civilization—if not by Huck then at least by Mark Twain.

The n-word has historically been intimately linked to slavery (the word was initially placed in front of a common American given name to distinguish the slave from any local white person with the same name). In addition, slavery and the Bible were intimately linked in early 19th century American culture, especially in the South. Samuel Clemens (Mark Twain's birth name) recalls that, in his boyhood town of Hannibal, Missouri—in which approximately 25% of the town's population were slaves—"The local pulpit taught us that God approved [of slavery], that it was a holy thing, and that the doubter need only look in the Bible if he wished to settle his mind—and then the texts were read aloud to us to make the matter sure."[3] In *Mark Twain's Religion*, author William Phipps cites two well-used New Testament texts for Southern Christians to justify their ways: "Servants, obey in all

---

[3] *The Autobiography of Mark Twain*, 2 vols., ed. Charles Neider (New York: Harper, 1990) 1:6.

things your masters," and "Let as many servants as are under the yoke count their own masters worthy of all honour."[4]

There was a rub, however, in many slaveholders' perceptions that African-American slaves were property (in effect, nonhuman or at least subhuman), which was that their slaves were indeed human, spiritual beings. According to Mark Twain scholar Michael Hearn,

> God-fearing Southern slave owners, who believed that the Bible sanctioned the "peculiar institution" [of slavery], considered it their responsibility to provide their servants with some religious instruction.... Sometimes [slaves] were taken to church, where they were segregated from their owners. "They had one corner where they sat with the slaves of other people," recalled Missouri slave Malinda Discus. "There was always something about that that I couldn't understand. They treated the colored folks like animals and would not hesitate to sell and separate them, yet they seemed to think they had souls and tried to make Christians of them."[5]

Even as a young child, Mark Twain thus witnessed in the moral landscape of his culture the shams and chicaneries and hypocrisies associated with anyone using religious language and sacred text to bolster certain political, economic, cultural, or personal wants and desires. Writes Phipps: "Unchristian deeds, not impious words, concerned MT [Mark Twain]; true blasphemy came from the hands, not the lips. Thus, much like Jesus, he criticized hypocrites who mouthed

---

[4] William Phipps, *Mark Twain's Religion* (Macon, GA: Mercer University Press, 2003) 28-29. NT texts are Colossians 3:22 and I Timothy 6:1.

[5] *The Annotated Huckleberry Finn*, 23n.29.

religious language but failed to reach out to help those in need."[6]

It is not a conceit, then, to link Missourian Sam Clemens's direct experiences with the pain and injustice of slavery to how American author Mark Twain takes aim throughout his writing career at both subtle and gross hypocrisies of those who use religion to mask their own shady ethical choices—choices, for instance, made by clans like the feuding Shepherdson and Grangerford families when they find themselves together at the same church each Sunday despite their ancient civil grudge. As Huck reports:

> Sunday we all went to church.... The men took their guns along... and kept them between their knees or stood them handy against the wall.... It was pretty ornery preaching—all about brotherly love, and such-like tiresomeness; but everybody said it was a good sermon, and they all talked it over going home, and had such a powerful lot to say about faith, and good works, and free grace, and preforeordestination, and I don't know what all, that it did seem to me to be one of the roughest Sundays I had run across yet. (Chap. 18)

What made the Sunday so rough for poor Huck? Huck's humorously unwitting conflation of the two Calvinist doctrines of predestination and foreordination is just the beginning. In addition, and according to Phipps, "the sermon on 'brotherly love' expresses the congregation's piety but not their practice, whereas such Christian love expresses Jim and Huck's practice but not their piety."[7]

---

[6] Phipps, 138.
[7] Phipps, 171.

In the next chapter, Huck and Jim are compelled take up for a time with two con men and shysters who call themselves the duke and the king, the latter of whom speaks to the former of all his shams, including how "Preachin's my line, too; and workin' camp-meetin's; and missionaryin' around" and how "layin' on o' hands" was his "best holt," meaning that faith healing was his best specialty (Chap. 19).

What is thus important to recognize in all of Mark Twain's writings and especially in *Huckleberry Finn*, according to Phipps, is this: Mark Twain's own home-grown and life-long knowledge and use "of biblical teaching to rebuke the practices of [pro-slavery] Christians sheds light on the meaning he gives 'religion.'"[8] In Mark Twain's case, just like in Søren Kierkegaard's case, there is the religion of New Testament Christianity and Christian doctrine on the one hand. On the other hand, there is a rogue brand of institutionalized religion identified by both authors as Christendom. Christendom is a manmade institution that may, for instance, endorse slavery and the unjust exploitation of any individual or group at the expense of the disenfranchised; it also may inordinately pad the pockets of its own ecclesiastical members instead of tend to the impoverished in its midst. Both Mark Twain and Kierkegaard were especially intent upon helping people who called themselves Christians examine themselves in ways that would elucidate gaps between what they preach and what they practice. In the end, the ethical truths have everything to do with being honest with oneself, with knowing oneself, with—in effect—becoming human. Both Mark Twain and Kierkegaard's works, in effect, hold a mirror up to the dual nature of the human self, to expose both the less

---

[8] Phipps, 36.

ethical side of human nature while occasionally offering examples of humans' more ethical side. Writes Kierkegaard:

> I very early was able to ascertain how seldom Christianity is presented in its true form, how those who defend it most often betray it, and how rarely the attackers actually hit it, although they often, which is still my view, superbly hit established Christendom, which certainly might rather be called the caricature of true Christianity.... My entire work as an author evolves around: becoming a Christian in Christendom."[9]

Or, as Mark Twain once wrote in a margin of a book: "The only really important question is, how to be a Christian yet not a fool."[10]

•

In his *Adventures of Huckleberry Finn*, however, Mark Twain begins his own attack upon the pro-slavery Christendom softly and humorously. *Huck Finn* is a narrative that, despite or because of how it masks itself as a children's book, also (and according to critic John Hays) "contains the seeds of all Clemens's religious thought."[11] It is a book, according to Phipps, in which "the struggle to rise above conventional values and to act justly is the basic religious issue."[12]

Below are three brief scenes in the book's early chapters that show how inconspicuously Mark Twain enters into the

---

[9] *The Point of View*, 80, 90 (XIII 565, 575).

[10] William Phipps, 374. Mark Twain's assertion is originally from Mark Twain's marginalia in his copy of Andrew White, *A History of the Warfare of Science with Theology* as noted in Alan Gribben's *Mark Twain's Library* (Boston: Hall, 1980) 760.

[11] John Hays, *Mark Twain and Religion* (New York: Lang, 1989) 122.

[12] Phipps, 169.

highly conspicuous religious issue of dehumanization through slavery in 19th century America:

Scene #1: "After supper [the Widow Douglas] got out her book and learned me about Moses and the Bulrushers, and I was in a sweat to find out all about him; but by-and-by she let it out that Moses had been dead a considerable long time; so then I didn't care no more about him; because I don't take no stock in dead people" (Chap. 1). Regarding this passage, Hearn notes that

> the widow wishes Huck to identify her with the Pharaoh's daughter who adopted the baby Moses. This casual reference to Exodus 2:3-10 introduces a central theme to the novel: Like Moses who freed the Israelites from bondage in Egypt, so too does Huck Finn aid a Southern slave in his flight from his master. Both outlawed boys escape by a river: Moses in an ark of bulrushes on the Nile, Huck by a raft down the Mississippi. And both are wards of women of the upper class, the slave-owning class. This scripture especially appealed to slaves who knew that one day they too would be liberated. "Go down, Moses!" they sang. "Tell old Pharaoh, let my people go!"[13]

Scene #2: "Then she [the Widow Douglas] told me all about the bad place [hell], and I said I wished I was there. She got mad, then, but I didn't mean no harm. All I wanted was to go somewheres; all I wanted was a change, I warn't particular. She said it was wicked to say what I said; said she wouldn't say it for the whole world; *she* was going to live so as to go to the good place [heaven]. Well, I couldn't see no advantage in where she was going, so I made up my mind I wouldn't try for it" (Chap. 1). This little scene establishes the basis of so much of Huck's climactic resolution in Chapter 31 to go to hell. If

---

[13] *The Annotated Huckleberry Finn*, 19n.15.

heaven is a pro-slavery place as reflected in the Southern conventional morality of the time, then hell is preferred.

Scene #3: From the outset of Chapter 3, the overly pious, conventional, and fearful Miss Watson tries to instruct Huck in the act of prayer. Failing miserably, she explains to Huck that one prays for "spiritual gifts," meaning, according to Huck, that "I must help other people, and do everything I could for other people, and look out for them all the time, and never think about myself.... I went out in the woods and turned it over in my mind a long time, but I couldn't see no advantage about it—except for the other people—so at last I reckoned I wouldn't worry about it any more, but just let it go" (Chap. 3). And despite Huck "letting it go," or perhaps because he does let it go, Huck helps his slave friend Jim later in the book—out of a sort of untainted and unknowing goodness. Miss Watson's moral lesson ultimately ends up being the most essential lesson that Huck practices in his relationship with Jim.

Two: "Telling the truth lying" (Mark Twain's humor)

Howard Hong writes that "man is uniquely characterized and profoundly defined as the being who laughs. Laughter arises essentially from an awareness of contradiction, opposites, basic contrasts.... between what is expected and what is, what is and what ought to be."[14] Add to this compact definition of laughter that Mark Twain's humor was primarily satirical, and some durable conclusions for *why* Mark Twain trafficked in humor is evident. For the best of satire reveals a society's trivial and terrible contradictions, hypocrisies, and absurdities. What ought to be versus what actually is in a society comes

[14] "The Comic, Satire, Irony, and Humor: Kierkegaardian Reflections," 99.

into bold relief...and humans laugh. Laughter, in other words, is the exclusively human expression that indicates that humans are aware on some level the ethical incongruity between what is and what ought to be.

The society of the duke and the king, for example, pretends to be something that it isn't. They are con men pretending to be earnest and genuine men, and readers' laughter exposes the con for the sham that it is. For laughter indicates that readers know right from wrong, truth from trash. Laughter indicates, in the end, that humans are at *heart* ethical beings—even though, most of the time, human *minds* forever scan the playing field to rationalize, justify, and excuse less ethical behaviors to avoid the hard task of ethical behavior.

In addition, the ethical purpose of great satire is to improve societies. Satire generally assumes that societies are more tribal and exclusive and self-interested than loving and inclusive and neighborly. Satire also assumes that societies generally see only what they want to see in the context of their members' self-interests instead of seeing how they may best exist in relation to members of other societies. In the end, satire seeks for the society upon which it serves its commentary a more comprehensive or biopic social vision that must thereby necessarily include a self-examination of the particular society's own myopic shortfalls, biases, and prejudices. Huck says it all in an even more fundamental way: "a body can see and don't see at the same time" (Chap. 34). Here, Huck unwittingly suggests that only by first ethically seeing and examining a society's own contradictions and blind spots may anybody within the society begin to make life better for everybody. Phipps further expands this notion, writing that Mark Twain's

> eagerness for social reform was motivated by his prophetic awareness of the painful difference between what a culture is and what it ought to be. A religious work often portrays a paradise to make the deficiencies of the present society stand out in bold relief. The gulf between the ideal and the actual provides incongruity on which much humor is based. His rejection of sordid society emerged from what he imagined a holy society to be. He embraced Isaiah's vision of a righteous and peaceful government and a restored Eden as well as that ancient preacher's condemnation of the phony unethical religion then practiced.[15]

Mark Twain even saw himself as a sort of preacher. "I have always preached," he writes. "If the humor came of its own accord and uninvited I have allowed it a place in my sermon, but I was not writing the sermon for the sake of the humor."[16]

If it seems a bit of a stretcher (Mark Twain's word for exaggeration) to consider Mark Twain as a preacher, it is noteworthy that he once said to a reporter that some people lie by pretending to tell the truth. But for Mark Twain: "I tell the truth lying."[17] He thus joins the ranks of humorist Søren Kierkegaard, who speaks of delivering the truth similarly. "One can deceive a person out of what is true," Kierkegaard writes, "and...one can deceive a person into what is true.... To be at all beneficial and not cause irreparable harm," Kierkegaard writes elsewhere, the well-meaning humorist "must have...a consistent and well-grounded ethical view...; otherwise the medicine [of humor] becomes infinitely worse

---

[15] Phipps, 367.

[16] *The Autobiography of Mark Twain*, 273.

[17] Phipps, 362 [quoted fr. *The Independent* (5 May 1910)].

than the sickness."[18] Mark Twain had this ethical view in his writings. And he, too, like Kierkegaard, treated humor as a border region between the ethical and the religious. Samuel Clemens as Mark Twain, in other words, could say along with one of Kierkegaard's own pen-names, "If I know nothing else, I do know that the comic ought to be used to keep order in the sphere of the religious."[19]

How does all this apply to Huck Finn?

In the first paragraph of his story, Huck says, "I never seen anybody but lied, one time or another" (Chap. 1). Yet Huck himself, according to Hearn, "never lies or steals for self-gain, only for self-preservation. And he never deceives himself: In his agonizing wrestling with his unrelenting conscience, he follows the honest dictates of his good heart"[20]—and he does this against all odds—against growing up poor; without a mother; and with an alcoholic, sometimes cruel, but mostly absent father. Huck, then, follows Mark Twain's rule about lying: "Lies told to injure a person, and lies told to profit yourself are not justifiable, but lies told to help another person, that is quite another matter."[21] Mark Twain's humor, of course, enters into the fray either to justify the ethical lie or to condemn the unethical lie.

In one dramatic yet still humorous scene, Mark Twain has Huck play out a lie that not only protects Jim, but also helps readers see Mark Twain's brand of ethical and ethical-

---

[18] *The Point of View*, 53 (XIII 541); Søren Kierkegaard, *Two Ages*, eds. and trs. Howard V. Hong and Edna H. Hong (Princeton: Princeton University Press, 1978) 74 (VIII 70).

[19] Søren Kierkegaard, *Stages on Life's Way*, eds. and trs. Howard V. Hong and Edna H. Hong (Princeton: Princeton University Press, 1988) 259 (VI 244).

[20] *The Annotated Huck Finn*, clviii.

[21] *Tales, Sketches et al. 1852-90*, 136.

religious humor in action. In this scene, Huck and Jim are on their raft going down the Mississippi River north of Cairo, Illinois near the confluence of the Mississippi and Ohio rivers. There, they plan to turn left and paddle up the Ohio to freedom. It's at that moment, however, that Huck realizes his disloyalty to his own pro-slavery conscience and heritage, and this grates on him. Nevertheless, Huck protects Jim by lying. Meanwhile, the humor of the scene shows readers not only the absurd contradictions of pro-slavery "Christian" bounty hunters, but also how Huck begins to grapple with the absurd contradictions implicit in his pro-slavery conscience and heritage.

> Jim said it made him all over trembly and feverish to be so close to freedom. Well, I can tell you it made me all over trembly and feverish, too, to hear him, because I begun to get it through my head that he *was* most free—and who was to blame for it? Why, *me*.... I tried to make out to myself that I warn't to blame, because *I* didn't run Jim off from his rightful owner; but it warn't no use, conscience up and says, every time, "But you knowed he was running for his freedom, and you could a paddled ashore and told somebody." That was so—I couldn't get around that, noway.

Jim then talks of his hopes and dreams of becoming free, which flabbergasts Huck: "I was sorry to hear Jim say that, it was such a lowering of him." Huck's pro-slavery conscience inspires him to paddle to shore and report Jim to authorities. Then Huck sees a light that may indicate their nearness to Cairo, and Jim yells:

> "We's safe, Huck, we's safe! Jump up and crack yo' heels!, dat's de good ole Cairo at las', I jis knows it!"
>
> I says:

> "I'll take the canoe and go and see, Jim. It mightn't be, you know...."
>
> I was paddling off, all in a sweat to tell on him; but when he says this, it seemed to kind of take the tuck all out of me.

When Huck is not far off from his destination, Jim says, "Dah you goes, de ole true Huck; de on'y white genlman dat ever kep' his promise to ole Jim"—which makes Huck feel terrible. At that moment, a skiff with two bounty hunters approach Huck, asking him about Jim and Huck's raft, now 50 yards off. When they ask if the man on it is black or white, Huck isn't quick to answer.

> I tried to, but the words wouldn't come. I tried for a second or two to brace up and out with it, but I warn't man enough—hadn't the spunk of a rabbit. I see I was weakening; so I just give up trying, and up and says—
>
> "He's white."

When the bounty hunters decide to see for themselves, Huck's lie is brilliantly stretched to the extent in which Huck actually *encourages* the men to investigate because

> "it's pap that's there, and maybe you'd help me tow the raft ashore where the light is. He's sick—and so is mam and Mary Ann."
>
> "Oh, the devil! we're in a hurry, boy. But I s'pose we've got to. Come, buckle to your paddle, and let's get along...."
>
> "Pap'll be mighty much obleeged to you, I can tell you. Everybody goes away when I want them to help me tow the raft ashore, and I can't do it by myself."
>
> "Well, that's infernal mean. Odd, too. Say, boy, what's the matter with your father?"

> "It's the—a—the—well, it ain't anything, much."
>
> They stopped pulling. It warn't but a mighty little ways to the raft now. One says:
>
> "Boy, that's a lie. What *is* the matter with your pap? Answer up square now, and it'll be the better for you."
>
> "I will, sir, I will, honest—but don't leave us, please. It's the—the—gentlemen, if you'll only pull ahead, and let me heave you the headline, you won't have to come a-near the raft—please do."
>
> "Set her back, John, set her back!" says one. They backed water.... Confound it, I just expect the wind has blowed it to us. Your pap's got the small-pox, and you know it precious well. Why didn't you come out and say so? Do you want to spread it all over?"
>
> "Well," says I, a-blubbering, "I've told everybody before, and they just went away and left us."

Then, after the men feel bad enough for the young boy and his poor family (enough to pass along to him two 20-dollar gold pieces), they depart. Meanwhile, the pro-slavery conscience of Huck gets the better of him again for a time

> because I knowed very well I had done wrong, and I see it warn't no use for me to try to learn to do right; a body that don't get *started* right when he's little ain't got no show—when the pinch comes there ain't nothing to back him up and keep him to his work, and so he gets beat. Then I thought a minute, and says to myself, hold on—s'pose you'd a done right and give Jim up, would you felt better than what you do now? No, says I, I'd feel bad—I'd feel just the same way I do now. Well, then, says I, what's the use you learning to do right when it's troublesome to do right and ain't no trouble to do wrong, and the wages is

> just the same? I was stuck.... So I reckoned I wouldn't bother no more about it, but after this always do whichever come handiest at the time. (Chap. 16)

In a copy of British novelist William Thackeray's essay on the great satirist Jonathan Swift, Mark Twain underlined what Thackeray writes about the religious purpose of humor: "'The humourous writer professes to awaken and direct your love, your pity, your kindness—your scorn for untruth, pretension, imposture—your tenderness for the weak, the poor, the unhappy.... He takes upon himself to be the week-day preacher.'" Phipps comments about this passage that "through humor, Thackeray and MT were able to entice the public to swallow the unpleasant truth and find in it a cure for their personal and corporate sins."[22]

But perhaps Mark Twain might be his own best critic regarding the humor of truth-telling by lying. For a men's church group of which Mark Twain was a member in Hartford, Connecticut, he writes in meeting notes: "Club subject—The insincerity of Man—all men are liars [Psalm 116:11], ...hiders of facts, half tellers of truths, shirks, moral sneaks. When a merely *honest* man appears he is a comet—his fame is eternal—Luther, Christ, and maybe God made two others—or one—besides me."[23]

Three: Huck's hell

At the town of Cairo, located at the southern tip of Illinois, the confluence of the Mississippi and Ohio rivers begins. Jim tells Huck that when "the two big rivers joined together there, that would show" (Chap. 16). As Mark Twain notes in *Life on*

[22] Phipps, 366.

[23] Phipps, 131 (*Mark Twain's Notebooks and Journals* (Berkeley: University of California Press, 3 vol., 1975-79) 3:144).

the Mississippi, "Ohio water didn't like to mix with Mississippi water," and that "if you take the Mississippi on a rise when the Ohio is low, you'll find a wide band of clear water all the way down the east side of the Mississippi for a hundred mile or more."[24]

In Jim and Huck's southbound Mississippi River rafting odyssey, then, Cairo is the point where clear water meets muddy, which is where they hoped to begin moving up the Ohio and into free states. But heavy nighttime fog coupled with other mishaps dashes this plan, and the black man and the white boy miss the turn. "When it was daylight," Huck writes, "here was the clear Ohio water in shore, sure enough, and outside was the old regular Muddy! So it was all up with Cairo" (Chap. 16). Subsequently, Huck and Jim seek to replace their lost canoe by buying another one, then abandon their raft, then paddle back upriver. But the next night, a steamboat smashes into Jim and Huck's raft, separating the two for a time. When they eventually reunite after Huck witnesses the ongoing civil strife between feuding Grangerford and Shepherdson families, their desire to flee to the north is further waylaid by being compelled to join up with two of the muddiest, slimiest bottom-feeders and inhumane humans in American literature. And not long after they meet with this "duke" and "king," they are far beyond the point where any clear Ohio water is visible any more. It's all Big Muddy as they continue to float deeper into slave states.

As the narrative unfolds south of Cairo, Huckleberry Finn begins to grow and mature in ways far beyond the boundaries of children's literature, for the intensely murky,

---

[24] Mark Twain, *Life on the Mississippi*, Chap. 3 (fr. *Mississippi Writings* (U.S.A.: Library of America, 1982) 245).

muddy 19th century American issues of race and civil strife and con men around every bend now loom frighteningly real.

In the context of Mark Twain's religion, this image of separate rivers—one low and clear and one on the rise and muddy before the former fully dissolves into the latter—is richly evocative. Even beyond the point at Cairo where the two rivers meet, they distinctly maintain their respective clear and muddy properties for a substantial stretch downriver before the clear is ultimately lost amid the dominant and prevailing currents of the "old regular Muddy," just as the innocence and honesty of youth is eventually lost in the murky currents of the human propensities for deception and self-deception that appear with age, intelligence, and experience.

If Huck's narrative may be regarded as what some critics have dubbed an "American Gospel" along the lines of New Testament Gospels, the narrative has something to do with floating deep into the rising flood of the "old regular Muddy" of life precisely because one can't be found until one becomes lost; then (in an effort to avoid surrendering to and being subsumed by the flood), the task is to understand how to reverse the trajectory and paddle toward some clearer discrimination between what is fundamentally clear and what is fundamentally muddy, *even if one forever paddles in what is fundamentally muddy*. Sacred or profane gospel narratives become particularly compelling when being found occurs after being lost, where the essence of goodness is consciously or unconsciously maintained amid an actuality of contagion.

Huck experiences this kind of enlightenment and this kind of courage. But Huck doesn't find these things until he's long lost sight of the well-defined distinctions between clear and muddy waters—not even until the climax, when Huck finds himself utterly lost to the world before unwittingly finding himself through a deep human connection he shares with Jim.

Before addressing the climax in detail, however, a few elements that combine to comprise the moral fog through which Huck navigates for a time are noteworthy.

There is the dominant and Muddy Mississippi River-like current of rational thought and egoism that swirls and churns in Huck's *head*—a forceful current that is dictated by a pro-slavery conscience. This conscience, nurtured by a provincial and bigoted cultural intelligence, never ceases to encourage Huck to subscribe to and continue the inherited cultural sin that emboldens a slave culture—a culture that goes so far as to call upon the language of the Bible and Christianity to come to its aid and protection. Then there is the less imposing and more naturally clear Ohio River-like flow of common ethical sense that moves through Huck's *heart*—a heart through which flows youthful life-blood waters of intuitive self-knowledge, self-examination, self-honesty, and simple faith in what is good.

Another element of this famous climax scene in American literature is something Mark Twain wrote elsewhere about slave property:

> In those slave-holding days the whole community was agreed as to one thing—the awful sacredness of slave property. To help steal a horse or a cow was a low crime, but to help a trusted slave or hesitate to promptly betray him to a slave-catcher when the opportunity offered was a much baser crime, and carried with it a stain, a moral smirch which nothing could wipe away.... It shows that that strange thing, the conscience—that unerring monitor—can be trained to approve any wild thing you

> *want* it to approve if you begin its education early and stick to it.[25]

Also, and despite Huck's aversion to the religious instruction presented to him by the Widow Douglas and Miss Watson, Huck's sense of Miss Watson's fire-and-brimstone image of hell is bred deeply into his being. This psychological inheritance must be fully appreciated to begin to understand the painful agony and the fearful, fearsome defiance informing his decision to go to hell for Jim's sake. In Huck's mind, this hell is real.

> I went to the raft, and set down in the wigwam to think. But I couldn't come to nothing. I thought till I wore my head sore, but I couldn't see no way out of the trouble. After all this long journey, and after all we'd done for them scoundrels [the duke and the king], here it was all come to nothing, everything all busted up and ruined, because they [the duke and the king] could have the heart to serve Jim such a trick as that, and make him a slave again all his life, and amongst strangers, too....

Huck then tries to convince himself that it would be better for Jim to be a slave back at home with his family, before realizing that Miss Watson might sell him for being a fugitive. Now that the thought of contacting Miss Watson has been raised, however, Huck's pro-slavery conscience, fueled by the pre-war Southern Christian morality, puts a stranglehold on Huck's better angel:

> The more I studied about this the more my conscience went to grinding me, and the more wicked and low-down and ornery I got to feeling. And at last, when it hit me all

---

[25] See Phipps, 170 (fr. *Mark Twain Papers*, notebook #35).

of a sudden that here was the plain hand of Providence slapping me in the face and letting me know my wickedness was being watched all the time from up there in heaven, whilst I was stealing a poor old woman's nigger that hadn't ever done me no harm, and now was showing me there's One that's always on the lookout, and ain't a-going to allow no such miserable doings to go only just so fur and no further, I most dropped in my tracks I was so scared. Well, I tried the best I could to kinder soften it up somehow for myself by saying I was brung up wicked, and so I warn't so much to blame; but something inside of me kept saying, "There was the Sunday school, you could a gone to it; and if you'd a done it they'd a learnt you there that people that acts as I'd been acting about that nigger goes to everlasting fire."

It made me shiver. And I about made up my mind to pray, and see if I couldn't try to quit being the kind of a boy I was, and be better. So I kneeled down. But the words wouldn't come. Why wouldn't they? It warn't no use to try and hide it from Him. Nor from *me*, neither. I knowed very well why they wouldn't come. It was because my heart warn't right; it was because I warn't square; it was because I was playing double. I was letting *on* to give up sin, but away inside of me I was holding on to the biggest one of all. I was trying to make my mouth *say* I would do the right thing and the clean thing, and go and write to that nigger's owner and tell where he was; but deep down in me I knowed it was a lie, and He knowed it. You can't pray a lie—I found that out.

So I was full of trouble, full as I could be; and didn't know what to do. At last I had an idea; and I says, I'll go and write the letter—and *then* see if I can pray. Why, it was astonishing, the way I felt as light as a feather right straight off, and my troubles all gone. So I got a piece of paper and a pencil, all glad and excited, and set down and wrote:

Miss Watson, your runaway nigger Jim is down here two mile below Pikesville, and Mr. Phelps has got him and he will give him up for the reward if you send.

HUCK FINN.

I felt good and all washed clean of sin for the first time I had ever felt so in my life, and I knowed I could pray now. But I didn't do it straight off, but laid the paper down and set there thinking—thinking how good it was all this happened so, and how near I come to being lost and going to hell. And went on thinking. And got to thinking over our trip down the river; and I see Jim before me all the time, in the day, and in the night-time, sometimes moonlight, sometimes storms, and we a-floating along, talking and singing and laughing. But somehow I couldn't seem to strike no places to harden me against him, but only the other kind. I'd see him standing my watch on top of his'n, stead of calling me, so I could go on sleeping; and see him how glad he was when I come back out of the fog; and when I come to him again in the swamp, up there where the feud was; and such-like times; and would always call me honey, and pet me and do everything he could think of for me, and how good he always was; and at last I struck the time I saved him by telling the men we had small-pox aboard, and he was so grateful, and said I was the best friend old Jim ever had in the world, and the *only* one he's got now; and then I happened to look around, and see that paper.

Then comes the climax:

> It was a close place. I took it up, and held it in my hand. I was a-trembling, because I'd got to decide, forever, betwixt two things, and I knowed it. I studied a minute, sort of holding my breath, and then says to myself:
>
> "All right, then, I'll *go* to hell"—and tore it up.
>
> It was awful thoughts and awful words, but they was said. And I let them stay said; and never thought no more about reforming. I shoved the whole thing out of my head, and said I would take up wickedness again, which was in my line, being brung up to it, and the other warn't. And for a starter I would go to work and steal Jim out of slavery again. (Chap. 31)

Despite Huck quickly growing up in this scene, his fundamental innocence is essential for the climax of the narrative to work as effectively as it does. And his innocence informs him that he failed to do what was the "right" thing to do, that he was behaving badly by saving Jim. As Phipps notes in scenes such as this, Mark Twain

> was attacking the kind of artificial morality that claimed bad behavior would necessarily result in poverty, illness, and early death. Recognizing that deity was not honored by lies, he thought religious characters should experience a mixture of failure and success, as was typical of Bible stories. Although he may not have been acquainted with the philosophy of Immanuel Kant, he discerned that true morality is doing what is right for its own sake, not for personal gain.[26]

---

[26] Phipps, 49.

What is also noteworthy is that it is hard to determine if Huck fully appreciates the kind of enlightenment and courage he experiences and suffers in the climax of the book. He is, after all, a boy. Consider, for instance, how easily Huck, ever inclined to take the path of least resistance unless doing otherwise is absolutely necessary, becomes a boy again for the last ten chapters of the book. All readers really know for certain about what Huck knows about himself by the last paragraph of his narrative is what readers learned about Huck in the second paragraph of Chapter 1, namely, his intolerance of a highly repressive, starched, whitewashed civilization and his intuitive need to break free of it by lighting out of it.

And readers may come to know one thing more that may hint of the kind of mature human being Huck may become long after his narrative ends. Huck always acts best when he first separates himself from others in order to think and reflect upon what is in his heart and also reflect upon words that may articulate what is in his heart—an act that many authentic religious leaders have famously done by first removing themselves to the wilderness or to some other monastic state for a time before re-emerging and continuing their ministry through deliberate deeds that are based upon a kind of deeply earnest reflection that ends in committed resolve. Perhaps Mark Twain was thinking of this particular habit of Huck's when he wrote to a devout Presbyterian and longtime friend of his: "One rational way of seeking Christ is to learn to put yourself out of sight when you are meditating an act, and consider how to do it for the comfort and benefit of others, and so take to itself a Christ-like spirit—and that bye and bye when one has made this a habit and it has become a pleasure to consider the weal of others first, that religion will not then be far away."[27]

In the end, putting oneself out of sight may be read two ways. Putting oneself out of sight first allows one the solitude and inwardness to think with reflection of one's more ethical nature from within. Second: it allows one to put one's own ego and self-interests out of sight to think more fully and thoughtfully of the needs of others.

And so the first moral lesson Miss Watson offers Huck in the narrative when she speaks to Huck of praying for "spiritual gifts" is made manifest, and is revealed in Huck's own words: "I must help other people, and do everything I could for other people, and look out for them all the time, and never think about myself." And even though Huck says he "went out in the woods and turned it over in [his] mind a long time, but [he] couldn't see no advantage about it—except for the other people" (Chap. 3), he nevertheless chooses to help his friend again and again, this black, this alien, this fugitive, this other, this neighbor, this wise and loving and generous Jim.

Four: Mark Twain's religion

In the climax of *The Adventures of Huckleberry Finn*, Huck makes a leap of faith more intensely than anywhere else in his narrative. He absolutely knows that his resolve to save Jim is wicked in his tribe's eyes and that, by extension of this inherited pro-slavery cultural sin, it is wicked in his own eyes. He absolutely knows, in effect, that his tribe will hate him for acting upon his resolve and he absolutely believes he will go to hell because of it. And yet, he also absolutely knows that,

---

[27] See Phipps, 84 (*Mark Twain's Letters* [Berkley: University of California Press, 6 vol., 1988-2002] 2:364).

before God, he can't "pray a lie" after he realized that his heart "warn't right" and "warn't square" with his pro-slavery head. He knew, in other words, he was "playing double"—he was in an unethical state of double-mindedness.

And even though true faith is blind, Huck's blind faith is not naïve, just as true obedience does not mean being a thoughtless, feckless follower of some unexamined code of conduct. Faith is most fully tested when human reliance on what the world wants is regularly doubted and challenged. If worldly rationalizations are found wanting, it is perhaps only an act of blind faith that abandons worldly human inclinations in deference to more ethical and ethical-religious dictates, like loving one's neighbor as one loves oneself.

Huck unwittingly comes to challenge and question instead of ignorantly rely upon his inherited pro-slavery conscience. When this conscience is found wanting, he comes to rely upon his free and more primitively ethical conscience and moral compass to do, whether he knows it or not at the time, the right thing—public opinion be damned. As Mark Twain writes, "a sound heart is a safer guide than an ill-trained conscience."[28]

But try telling that to the court of public opinion. In its unwavering support of worldly culture and civilization that is its highly coveted inheritance and legacy (no matter how decadent that culture and civilization is), public opinion may never see fit to allow the likes of Huckleberry Finn off the hook for going against its codes. In other words, no matter how readers may love and sympathize with and root for Huck Finn, most do so privately or in book groups or classrooms, for Huck's alternative code of behavior may not really be the code of behavior that most of its members may wish for their

---

[28] See Phipps, 173 (*Mark Twain Papers*, notebook #35).

children. Rather, most members of the culture want and wish for their children to grow up and become more like Tom Sawyer, because it's the pragmatic and opportunity-driven Tom Sawyers of the world, and not the Hucks of the world, who become teachers and lawyers and doctors and realtors and politicians and shopkeepers and retailers and heads of chambers of commerce. The Tom Sawyers of the world are not bad people, but they're also not Huck—Huck, who, at best, exists on the edge of each of the hearts and sympathies of the Tom Sawyers of the world.[29]

---

[29] Mark Twain makes this point abundantly clear when Huck is first introduced to the reading public in Mark Twain's *The Adventures of Tom Sawyer*: "Shortly Tom came upon the juvenile pariah of the village, Huckleberry Finn, son of the town drunkard. Huckleberry was cordially hated and dreaded by all the mothers of the town, because he was idle, and lawless, and vulgar and bad—and because all their children admired him so, and delighted in his forbidden society, and wished they dared to be like him. Tom was like the rest of the respectable boys, in that he envied Huckleberry his gaudy outcast condition, and was under strict orders not to play with him. So he played with him every time he got the chance. Huckleberry was always dressed in the cast-off clothes of full-grown men.... [and he] came and went, at his own free will. He slept on doorsteps in fine weather and in empty hogsheads in wet; he did not have to go to school or to church, or call any being master or obey anybody; he could go fishing or swimming when and where he chose, and stay as long as it suited him; nobody forbade him to fight; he could sit up late as he pleased; he was always the first boy that went barefoot in the spring and the last to resume leather in the fall; he never had to wash, nor put on clean clothes; he could swear wonderfully. In a word, everything that goes to make life precious, that boy had. So thought every harassed, hampered, respectable boy in St. Petersburg" (Mark Twain, *The Adventures of Tom Sawyer,* Chap. 6 (fr. *Mississippi Writings* (U.S.A.: Library of America, 1982) 45.

The seeds of Mark Twain's ethics and religion as well as his most beloved character, Huck Finn, are thus sown in a far more primitive ground of New Testament Christianity, one that is based upon free will and the courage to reject cultures that are at least tainted if not wholly dominated by corruption, hypocrisy, and chicanery—a ground that may prompt an individual to light out for better territory ahead of the rest.[30] Even if Huck ultimately elected not to exercise the pull toward being a hermit and flee from the world, perhaps he would have seen fit to, as Kierkegaard notes, "remain in the world to suffer for the truth."[31] Perhaps he would have found himself living *in* the world but not being *of* the world, not being subsumed or swallowed by the world but rather floating atop its muddy waters—as he always has. For this is what it means to be and become a human being, and also to be and become, as Mark Twain says, a Christian and yet not a fool.[32]

In the end, Huck is an ethicist despite himself. He may always be lonesome (he talks quietly and profoundly about feeling lonesome several times in the book[33]) and he may always be an outcast in the world of conventional pro-slavery morality that the respected elders of his community consider to be congruent with Christian morality. He also will be lonesome and an outcast in the decadent world of his father. But for Huck, buying into either culture is selling out. And so he becomes the poster child for Mark Twain's adage, "Be good and you will be lonesome."[34]

---

[30] See penultimate sentence of the novel.

[31] *Journals and Papers* 2:324 (X^2 A 326, n.d. 1849).

[32] See p. 14n. 10.

[33] See, e.g., chaps. 8, 15, 19, and 32.

[34] Mark Twain, *Following the Equator: A Journey Around the World* (Hartford: American Publishing Company, 1898). The

What does it thereby really mean to be, to become a human being? It means in great part being ethical. But to be an ethical human being in cultures tainted or dominated by a lack of ethics means to be a person who exposes the deceptions and self-deceptions of the culture and thereby appears to the culture as offensive, even obscene. British novelist Samuel Butler wrote that "people in general are equally horrified at hearing the Christian religion doubted, *and at seeing it practiced*"[35] [emphasis added]. Phipps adds: "Disturbed by the chasm between the profession and the practice of faith, MT strove to close the gap by focusing upon the ethical implications of Christianity."[36]

The ethicist-truth-teller, according to Kierkegaard, is not only undesirable and an affront but also hated and treated as an outcast, for the high standards to which the ethicist aspires are also standards of which all striving human beings are capable but that the vast majority of people resist.[37]

And so goodness and lonesomeness are indeed related, and it sometimes feels like it is just Huck and Jim against the whole world. Yet during the times they are alone together on Jackson's Island or their Mississippi raft, there is a simple,

---

caption is handwritten and signed by Mark Twain under a photograph of him sitting on shipboard following the title page.

[35] *Samuel Butler's Notebooks* (New York: Dutton, 1951) 310.

[36] Phipps, 359.

[37] See, e.g., *Journals and Papers* 1:376 (X^4 A 580, n.d. 1852); 408-409 (VII^1 A 28, n.d. 1846); 409 (VII^1 A 30, n.d. 1846); 417 (VIII^1 A 398, n.d. 1847); 418-19 (VIII^1 A 671, n.d. 1848); 424-25 (X^1 A 393, n.d. 1849); 431-32 (X^3 A 104, n.d. 1850); *Journals and Papers* 2:305 (XI^2 A 271, n.d. 1855); *Journals and Papers* 4:290-91 (VIII^1 A 160, n.d. 1847); *Journals and Papers* 6:473 (X^5 A 104, 25 March 1853 [Good Friday]).

direct, truthful, innocent, free quality about them that mimics the innocence of Adam himself before the Fall.

Their primary relationship, then, is also equally symbolic here. The moment before Huck first sees Jim in the narrative, it is midnight and Huck trips over a root, which compels Jim to call out "Who's there?" Thus begins a shared existence of simple innocence and blind faith even as they float through a world of complicated corruption and inscrutable machinations; it is precisely the primitive roots of goodness that trip up the civilized, just as the radical or "root" revelations of truth trip up the deceitful appearances of civilized, respectable, cultured society.

In Chapter 8, Huck is the American Adam on Jackson's Island:

> I went exploring around down through the island. I was boss of it; it all belonged to me, so to say, and I wanted to know all about it; but mainly I wanted to put in the time. I found plenty strawberries, ripe and prime; and green summer-grapes, and green razberries; and the green blackberries was just beginning to show.... I had my own gun along, but I hadn't shot nothing; it was for protection.... About this time I mighty near stepped on a good sized snake, and it went sliding off through the grass and flowers, and I after it, trying to get a shot at it. (Chap. 8)

In Chap. 19, Huck speaks of him and Jim rafting "naked, day and night, whenever the mosquitoes would let us," the new clothes he received from the Grangerfords "was too good to be comfortable."

Phipps notes that critic Lionel Trilling "provides a helpful analogy for examining the novel's [ethical and] religious meaning, 'The boy and the Negro slave form a family, a primitive community—and it is a community of saints.' There is depravity all along the river—hypocrisy, slavery, feudings, lynchings, murders—but the two on the raft represent the true church—compassion, forgiveness, loyalty, equality, and freedom.... The companionship of Huck and Jim on the river provides liberation from bigoted religion."[38]

[38] Phipps, 171 (Lionel Trilling, *Liberal Imagination* [NY: Viking, 1950] 108).

2

The Other in Herman Melville's *Moby-Dick*[1]

One: "Who aint a slave? Tell me that."

The opening 23 "shore" chapters of *Moby-Dick*, by Herman Melville (1819-91), are often quickly passed over by readers eager to get to the tale of Captain Ahab, the tyrannical, monomaniacal tragic hero who, while seeking oil in the commercial whaling industry on the seven seas, has his leg bitten off by a huge white sperm whale. Although advertised on shore as a commercial whaling venture so as to recruit a needed crew, the real goal of Ahab's next and final cruise is his own, made clear only after the ship is far out to sea. Most of *Moby-Dick* thus chronicles this particular war waged on behalf of a terror-filled and fearful personal vengeance, highlighting Ahab's puritanical brand of radical pessimism, his capability to turn the religious into the demonic, his isolated independence, his massive selfishness, his corrupt political will, and his sense of extravagant justice. Interestingly, Ahab doesn't even step on deck of his fated whaler until Chapter 29 of the 135-chapter

[1] Herman Melville, *Moby-Dick*, as published in the Northwestern-Newberry edition of *The Writings of Herman Melville*, vol. 6, ed. Harrison Hayford (Chicago: Northwestern University Press, 1988). Chapter numbers will be cited following quoted passages. Portions of this chapter were revised and included in *Sober Cannibals, Drunken Christians: Melville, Kierkegaard, and Tragic Optimism in Polarized Worlds* (Macon, GA: Mercer University Press, 2010).

novel. Before that appearance, two unsung heroes are the focus of the novel. Serving as healthy counterpoints to Ahab's isolationist monomaniacism, whalers Ishmael and Queequeg show how becoming human has something to do with understanding the human as a relational being whose primary task is to connect with and embrace "the other"—which is the focus of this chapter.

Moby-Dick's narrator, Ishmael, calls himself a "good Christian; born and bred in the bosom of the infallible Presbyterian Church" (Chap. 1). He also is an ex-school teacher who "loves to sail forbidden seas" and intends to ship out as a "greenhorn" whaler. While preparing departure from New Bedford, Massachusetts, he crosses paths with Queequeg, a pagan idolater and a cannibal. Together, they explore and actualize the possibilities of a uniquely American *and* essentially Christian spirit predicated on mutually dependent love, mercy, forgiveness, and understanding of the other. Ishmael and Queequeg's relationship subsequently results in a happy marriage of Christian and non-Christian thought. And although this part of the story is quickly driven deep beneath the waves of Ahab's vengeful prow for most of the remainder of the novel, its presence at the beginning of the book serves as the only viable and healthy alternative to Ahab's tragically narrow, one-sided, and ultimately suicidal world-view. Ishmael and Queequeg's relationship succeeds insofar as it survives not by the denial of or resistance to diversity, but rather by embracing the alien, the stranger, the outcast, the other. These early chapters thus embody critical wisdom of the dynamics between preaching and practicing Christian ethics in a conventional Christendom that tries to sustain itself amid an increasingly pluralistic American culture. In addition, these chapters offer some of the finest examples in American literature of satire and comic insight into the contradiction between conventional piety and fundamental Christian ethics.

•

A happy marriage between Christianity and cultural diversity exists in Melville's novel. That said, there's nothing really "happy" about either marriage or about confronting issues of diversity—if "happiness" is defined as a static and unthinking contentment sustained over time. When, for instance, we conclude about most marriages that "the honeymoon is over," then presumably the "happy" gift of the initial romance has expired with the advent of the actual task of sustaining a marriage. Or when we say that cultural diversity must be "embraced" or "celebrated," we may romantically imply that the embrace or celebration is welcome and "happy." But embracing or celebrating diversity is really nothing more nor less than hard work; the act of such embrace, implying close intimacy, assaults a sense of tribal instinct that dictates members only embrace that which is *like* them. The thought of embracing something alien, much less happily celebrating it, threatens the tribal member's loyalty that exists to protect the integrity of the member's tribe—for "diversity" is code for "the other," the other side of an argument, and other people who live on the other side of the tracks or the other side of town. Natural instincts influence us only to embrace what is like us, whereas Christian neighbor-love ethics indicate the opposite, namely, that we embrace the other, that which is not like us.

If, however, happiness is defined not as a state of static satisfaction or contentment with the known but rather as a movement toward the unknown (*movement toward* being the operative descriptor for a more dynamic and sustainable sense of happiness), then embracing diversity or the post-honeymoon part of a marriage are indeed happy events. To do this, however, requires admitting to oneself that one's own ignorance about oneself and the world and time are wider and more varied than what one does know or think one knows about oneself and the world and time. And herein lies the rub, for the thought of admitting ignorance offends many people's egos, which, in turn, inclines most individuals to harbor their ignorance instead of suffer what is revelatory and educational.

But still: why is it that humans have such a difficult time embracing diversity, that idea of "otherness"—the otherness in ourselves and others? If what novelist William Faulkner says about true love is correct—that we love not *because* but *despite*[2]—then to love means to embrace others despite fears that lurk in the shadows of the other, despite issues of diversity or differences, and despite what we may think to be others' flaws.

Given years of debates (especially in the United States) over gay marriage and issues of diversity ranging from immigration policies to the ethics of flag burning to whether or not we ought to define the U.S. as a Christian nation to whether or not (if we are labeled a Christian nation) we ought to treat Muslims or Arabs or Jews or Palestinians as we treat ourselves or to whether or not we ought to love our enemies (diversity's ultimate embrace of the "other");—given all of these difficulties surrounding the words "marriage" and "diversity," it is hard to talk of diversity in the conventionally common, romantic, esthetic, static meaning of the term "happiness." And yet, Melville shows both the possibility and the actuality of a more authentic happiness and love in the shore chapters of

---

[2] *Holiday Magazine* (Philadelphia: Curtis Publishing Co., April 1954). Also quoted in "Faulkner's Mississippi," by Willie Morris in *National Geographic* (March 1989) 336.

Moby-Dick—if "happiness" is defined as being a movement toward the other.

In the case of Ishmael, the initial terror of relating himself to himself and moving towards others is intimately personal and unsentimentally a matter of life and death. In addition, his otherwise unassuming New Bedford and Nantucket rambles spawn arduous challenges to his provincial sensibilities and to the conventional, self-enclosed Christian morality by which he was raised within "an old established family in the land" (Chap. 1). Further: Ishmael summons up significant references to both Old and New Testaments—references that foreshadow the terrifying fire and brimstone of Captain Ahab as much as they offer calming revelatory news of radical goodness.

Of the earnestness by which readers are called upon to embrace Ishmael's critical humor that satirizes Christendom while simultaneously endorsing fundamental Christian ethics, two comments by Melville to fellow author Nathaniel Hawthorne are worth mentioning. In a comment correctly forecasting the negative critical reception and poor financial remuneration Melville would receive from his nearly completed novel, *Moby-Dick*, Melville writes: "Though I wrote the Gospels in this century, I should die in the gutter."[3] After *Moby-Dick*'s publication, Melville writes to Hawthorne again: "I have written a wicked book, and feel spotless as a lamb."[4] Of this last passage, Melville's most thorough biographer, Hershel Parker, notes that Melville called his book "wicked" in

---

[3] *Correspondence*, ed. Lynn Horth (vol. 14 of the Northwestern-Newberry edition of *The Writings of Herman Melville* (Chicago: Northwestern University Press, 1993)) 192 ([June 1?], 1851).

[4] *Correspondence*, 192 ([November 17], 1851).

part because *Moby-Dick* "challenged conventional American piety."[5]

Given the earnestness of Melville's thoughts on religion in a time when he witnessed much religious hypocrisy, and given his experience that the world did not in his lifetime recognize or appreciate his genius, Melville understood the role of outcast—which brings us to the first three words of the novel: "Call me Ishmael."

These three words frame the entire book. They suggest that the person owning the name exists essentially separate from the world even while living in the world—and Melville wants us not only to call the narrator of his book Ishmael, he wants us to come to sympathize with his narrator in such a way that we may come to assume the experience of this stranger and outcast as our own. Add the notion that Melville's narrator also prefers to remain anonymous (we never know if Ishmael is his actual name) and we have a human stripped to the bare bones of human identity—identity that more commonly and conventionally is founded upon a given name and lineage. Given, then, that the spiritual ancestor of Melville's narrator is the Old Testament's poster child for Outcast, Melville suggests the currency of our true selves is foreign currency outside of Eden and thus worth nothing. British poet John Milton's last words of *Paradise Lost* describing Adam and Eve as representatives of all humanity for all time, are terrifying: "They hand in hand with wand'ring steps and slow/Through Eden took their solitary way."[6] Two similar lines from Emily Dickinson also terriffy: "Parting is all

---

[5] Hershel Parker, *Herman Melville: A Biography*, vol. 2 (Baltimore: The Johns Hopkins University Press, 1996) 15.

[6] John Milton, *Complete Poetry and Major Prose*, ed. Merritt Y. Hughes (Indianapolis: Odyssey Press, 1957) fr. *Paradise Lost* 12.648-49.

we know of heaven,/And all we need of hell."[7] A line from Søren Kierkegaard's journals also terrifies: "When *an existence* is genuinely considered *under the aspect of the eternal, the result is*, eo ipso [thereby], *isolation*."[8]

Ishmael is thereby the name we think of when we think of one who is outcast or separated or isolated from the whole. And so what better name could Melville have given his narrator—a narrator with whom Melville immediately wants us all to identify and sympathize? By casting the narrator out on the periphery of his culture, Melville also endows Ishmael with the capability of formulating a more objective and thereby potentially more truthful and unbiased view of that culture. In other words, unlike loyal and unreflective insiders, partisans, or patriots, Ishmael is free from toeing any given party-line.

Ishmael is not solely dependent upon the culture for financial advancement or a way of life, so he is more able to speak honestly, either well or ill, about the culture. His words may even hold greater credibility because he also is not quite out of the culture by virtue of his shared history with it. In addition, his words are credible because of his self-effacing humor—humor that regularly confesses his own prejudices before seeking ways to correct and balance himself while indirectly helping us on our own journeys by prompting us to examine ourselves similarly.

At the least, Ishmael's peripheral existence in relation to his culture informs his ultimate *physical* survival. Ishmael claims that the whaling ship (pregnantly named *Rachel*) had merely "found another orphan" when it ladled him out of the

---

[7] Emily Dickinson, *Final Harvest: Emily Dickinson's Poems*, ed. Thomas H. Johnson (Boston: Little, Brown, and Co., 1961) #1732.

[8] *Journals and Papers* 1:451 (VI A 65, n.d. 1845).

ocean at the end of the novel. Ishmael survives the wreckage of the *Pequod*, however, by being on the periphery and edge of that culture after having been cast out of one of the *Pequod*'s doomed whaleboats—a whaleboat that also gets "drawn towards" and ultimately surrenders to "the closing vortex" (Epilogue) of the culture that built and steered it. Ishmael alone survives to tell the tale by not being wholly a part of the group but by being an outcast and orphan, whether by chance, choice, or fate. As an individual outside the culture, he is (perhaps ironically) capable of being a more integrated self on deeper psychological, emotional, and spiritual levels than a person who signs away much individuality by becoming a more or less anonymous part of a greater whole. As for what Ishmael comes to call himself and his shipmates—*isolatos*—he resists becoming one who is used and possibly abused by a larger culture, but by doing so he subsequently rejects the worldly securities that the society offers its partisans.

The outcast, however, thus need not exclude an ethical component that innately informs all individuals inside or outside a social fabric. In the first chapter of *Moby-Dick*, Ishmael may consider himself a "wild man" akin to his Old Testament namesake, but perhaps only to the extent that he claims to "love to sail forbidden seas." Such a passion for what is forbidden is code for the human bent toward transgression, and for repeating the "sin" of the original "orchard thieves" (Chap. 1) by eating of forbidden fruit. Immediately after this bold confession of loving the forbidden, however, Ishmael writes perhaps the most significant ethical maxim of the book: "Not ignoring what is good, I am quick to perceive a horror, and could still be social with it—would they let me—since it is but well to be on friendly terms with all the inmates of the place one lodges in" (Chap. 1).

This ethical adage allows Ishmael to question and doubt conventional western morality that is more provincial than it perhaps represents itself as; the adage also allows Ishmael to question and to doubt that brand of "righteousness" that is more exclusive than inclusive. Ishmael's instinctive, implied ethical goal is to come to sympathize with, feel compassion for, and, in a phrase, love his neighbor. He understands both good and evil and denies neither. He knows he can, like the famous monkeys striking postures of willful ignorance, choose not to see nor hear nor speak evil. He also knows, however, that one does not deepen and mature in wisdom and truth or move toward healthy relationships if one ignores both real horrors and merely apparent horrors perceived out of ignorance and fear. In other words, not ignoring what is good but also not ignoring acquaintance with the alien, the strange, the apparently horrifying and reprehensible, the outcast, the minority, the disenfranchised, the neighbor—in a word, not ignoring the other—is part of the base of any Judeo-Christian ethic, an ethic embedded in the second love commandment that, along with the first love commandment, "hang all the law and all the prophets."[9]

Regarding issues of diversity, obeying the second love commandment (to love the neighbor as one loves oneself) also renders an individual more integrated into the whole in such a way that neither the self nor the whole diminishes the other because the self has the other in mind. This is perhaps what Ishmael means when he says in Chapter 1 that "It is quite as much as I can do to take care of myself," for when Ishmael listens to others, he both gains distance from himself to examine himself while simultaneously attending to the ethical being in himself that is called upon to serve others by at least

[9] Matthew 22:39-40.

respecting them, if not wholly agreeing with them. In the opening paragraphs of Chapter 1, Ishmael recognizes that selfishly denying the other and thus summarily rejecting the diversity that the other brings to a relationship renders his life less than what it can be, and thus he knows from the outset the feeling of depressive despair bordering on suicide. It is a despair that has, in the past, forced him to ask Hamlet's famous question: To be or not to be. How he humorously states this famous and overwhelming question of life or death only thinly masks the despair that all humans feel at some level. It is a spiritual despair of separation that finds its root in the self's misrelationship to itself and to others; it is a despair that nonetheless begins the real journey and first chapter of becoming more fully human:

> Whenever I find myself growing grim about the mouth; whenever it is a damp, drizzly November in my soul; whenever I find myself involuntarily pausing before coffin warehouses, and bring up the rear of every funeral I meet; and especially whenever my hypos get such an upper hand of me, that it requires a strong moral principle to prevent me from deliberately stepping into the street, and methodically knocking people's hats off—then, I account it high time to get to sea as soon as I can. This is my substitute for pistol and ball. With a philosophical flourish Cato throws himself upon his sword; I quietly take to the ship. There is nothing surprising in this. If they but knew it, almost all men in their degree, some time or other, cherish very nearly the same feeling towards the ocean with me. (Chap. 1)

Ishmael's life journey in this book is subsequently a journey of becoming human by mending the self amid a world of separations induced by selfishness. It is a journey from a depressed, egotistic, selfish place in which a self naturally inhabits, to a full, gracious, giving place of the self that is, to quote from Milton's *Paradise Lost*, "a paradise within thee, happier far."[10] Therefore, "the key to it all," according to Ishmael himself, is the story of Narcissus, a story of the search for a true self, a story in which "meditation and water are wedded for ever" (Chapter 1).

On each page, however, we find Ishmael both seriously and humorously examining his and every other characters' daily behaviors, prejudices, and acts of selfishness. Ishmael demonstrates early in the book what he states outright in Chapter 17, namely, that "we are all somehow dreadfully cracked in the head and sadly need mending." Ishmael makes light of hypochondria, suicide, selfishness, servitude, and boring workaday existences to level the playing field. "Who aint a slave? Tell me that," Ishmael asks in Chapter 1. And by that question, Ishmael immediately sympathizes with and is nonjudgmental toward the lonely plight of any individual human being, slave or king. In other words, when "weighed against" what Ishmael calls "the scales of the New Testament" (Chapter 1), the "indignity" of a simple sailor's servitude is not unlike the indignity of an inflated Commodore, and that *how* an individual ethically chooses to act toward him- or herself and toward others will determine that person's worth and character.

That said, Ishmael reserves the right and freedom of thought to be highly skeptical and humorously critical of man-made systems—not excluding institutionalized religion. He believes that only through the suffering heart of the single individual amid the discomfort of relating to others *without mediation* (instead of relating to others exclusively through

[10] *Paradise Lost*, 12.587.

social institutions that may dull or diminish the sovereignty of the individual heart and conscience) does a self come to know on what rock he or she stands.

Two: The self as relational phenomenon

At about the same time Melville begins composition of *Moby-Dick*, Kierkegaard suggests in opening paragraphs to his book *The Sickness Unto Death* the idea that the self is, at its heart, a relational phenomenon. Kierkegaard's idea illuminates Melville's strikingly similar concept of the self as a relational being.

A human being is spirit, Kierkegaard writes; and a human spirit is a human self; and a human self is a relation that relates itself to itself (we are, in other words, self-conscious beings). As a self-conscious being, the human self also relates itself to the other—this "other" existing either inside the self (for instance, one's conscience) or outside of the self.[11] If the "other" is outside the self, it may take on any number of forms, from human forms (for instance, a human friend, enemy, neighbor, or lover) to mythological forms (for instance, Greek gods) to natural forms (a whale) to manmade forms (a whaling ship) to divine forms (for instance, a transcendent power). From the standpoint of the essentially Christian self, the *other* ultimately exists to complete the fundamental self. In addition, a self exists more fully when it is in healthy relationships instead of misrelationships with others. In some of Kierkegaard's most algebraic phrasing—phrasing that (to borrow words from Ishmael) is apparently so "boggy, soggy, squitchy" that it is "enough to drive a nervous man distracted" (Chap. 3)—Kierkegaard concludes the opening paragraphs of

[11] See Søren Kierkegaard, *The Sickness Unto Death*, eds. and trs. Howard V. Hong and Edna H. Hong (Princeton: Princeton University Press, 1980) 14-15 (XI 127-28).

The Sickness Unto Death with this sentence: "The formula that describes the state of the self when despair is completely rooted out is this: in relating itself to itself and in willing to be itself, the self rests transparently in the power that established it."[12]

Similarly (and as suggested earlier), Ishmael suggests that "the key to it all" ("it" being "life" or "the self" or Ishmael's story about the life of human selves) is the *relational* phenomenon of life that humans envision when they look into the water and relate themselves to what they see everyday in the watery self-conscious mirror of their lives. Given Ishmael's claim that "meditation and water are wedded for ever" (Chap. 1), the "key to it all" is how humans reflectively engage or examine this reflection of themselves and *also* how, after reflection, humans choose or do not choose to strive ethically toward healthy relationships with this ever-fluid image of themselves and with others. In a nutshell, Ishmael's "key to it all" is how each individual inwardly and outwardly manages his or her watery, slippery, selfish self.

After discussing a romantic landscape painting that has a river run through it, and after posing five times the question of why water attracts human beings to it, Ishmael writes in Chapter 1: "And still deeper the meaning of that story of Narcissus, who because he could not grasp the tormenting, mild image he saw in the fountain, plunged into it and was drowned. But that same image," Ishmael concludes, "we ourselves see in all rivers and oceans. It is the image of the ungraspable phantom of life; and this is the key to it all." Given Ishmael's mention of the suicidal tale of the archetypal mythological narcissist, Ishmael's question regarding "the key to it all" fast becomes a question of death and life—death if we

---

[12] *The Sickness Unto Death*, 15 (XI 128).

consider only our narcissistic selves, life if we consider "the other."

The question of how the lost, narcissistic self journeys into itself to find or lose itself is ultimately Ishmael asking Hamlet's intimately human question: "To be or not to be…." —And if the "key to it all" (which presumably includes a life-affirming answer to the question of whether to live or die) has something to do with the issues of self, selfishness, self-reflection, and the self's relating itself to itself and others, then this self-reflective self must be addressed and applied to others whom Ishmael meets along his way.

There is, nevertheless, terrific irony that must be addressed in that there are precious few *others* whom Ishmael meets along the way who aren't men. This virtual absence of women in the book needs to be regarded as representative of the kind of radical imbalance, selfishness, and prejudice that is soon to emerge from below deck of the *Pequod* after the ship loses sight of Nantucket's sandy maternal shores.

It is, in addition, fitting that Melville names the only woman who has direct contact and business with the *Pequod* Charity, because if the *Pequod*'s final voyage will need anything, it will need what it will be sorely shown to lack, namely, charity (Chaps. 20, 22).

Aunt Charity is in charge of housekeeping on the *Pequod* before its departure, and she makes sure the ship is rigged out with everything that it needs for the long voyage, including a jar of pickles, a bunch of quill pens, a roll of flannel for the small of someone's rheumatic back, and a night-cap for her brother-in-law and second mate, Stubb. The final item she secures for the ship is a spare Bible. Ishmael speaks of Aunt Charity "charitably" and with a great and thankful kindness.

Melville critic John Parke addresses the notion of women and *Moby-Dick* when he writes that

> While it is of course fitting, or at least traditional, that hazardous expeditions are for men, the absence of women and their influence from the crew and, generally speaking, from the story, may be taken as symbolic. For not merely humanity (the moral quality) is left ashore, but the specific feminine principle of relatedness, of nurturing, of instinctive affection, is implicitly and expressly denied.... Masculinity is isolated; life is unbalanced.[13]

Parke's commentary here is important, for it makes the case that *Moby-Dick* is as much about the need for women and stereotypically feminine principles of connectedness and concern for the other than it is about the need for men and the stereotypically masculine principles of solitude and independence. Connectedness and concern for others (on the one hand) and solitude and independence (on the other) are equally good things when they are practiced in balance and in concert with the other. If, however, the self is primarily a relational phenomenon, and that the *other* ultimately serves to complete that which we call the self, then we are the most that our selves can be when we are in healthy relationship instead of isolated misrelationship with not only ourselves, but also others.

Before moving toward these particular relationships, however, a reminder: although the opening chapters of *Moby-Dick* offer some of the funniest chapters in American literature, they are also deeply earnest and pathos-filled, and what makes these chapters so funny is also what makes the pathos so poignant. For both Melville and Kierkegaard knew that all humor is based upon exposed and potentially painful human contradictions. Both also knew that, if humor offers an ethical

[13] John Parke, "Seven Moby Dicks," *New England Quarterly*, v.28, September 1955) 325-27.

component (and much humor has such a component), then the human contradictions we laugh at are presented in such a way that we may also laugh at ourselves. And if we are capable of laughing at ourselves, our laughter may be sufficient evidence that we see certain faults, errors, flaws, and contradictions in ourselves. And if we see *that*, we understand that, ethically, we may change our lives. Laughter directed at ourselves, in this sense, is evidence that there is an ethical being in ourselves gently transforming lesser selves into truer selves. All we need to effect such change is tears or pain or suffering or guilt at the witnessing of such contradictions, for tears or pain or suffering or guilt are sometimes the only reliable ethical agents for human change. If we should feel pain in the presence of wrongdoing, it may be because pain is more often than not an effective agent to mobilize ethical action to remedy the wrongdoing.

Such an ethical concept of pain and suffering also informs great literature to the point of being the mark that distinguishes great literature from merely good literature. Great literature—for instance, the Bible, Thoreau's *Walden*, Twain's *Huckleberry Finn*, Homer's *Iliad*, Shakespeare's plays, Dante's *Divine Comedy*, Dostoevsky's *The Brothers Karamazov*, Ibsen's *Peer Gynt*, Melville's *Moby-Dick*—is transformative literature. Such literature is a conduit through which people may change themselves or prepare themselves to be changed. But for great literature to be such a transformative agent, it must apply *pressure* to effect transformation. It must, in other words, be abrasive, so that readers become compelled to respond to the pressure. It must be uncomfortable; ethically, we are to commit ourselves to the uncomfortable nature of great books lest we, like those famous monkeys, choose not to see or speak or hear of corruptions or misdeeds that surround us—corruptions or misdeeds that might nonetheless make us more fully human if we first allow ourselves to recognize them.

Great literature is thus not unlike what Father Mapple calls "unwelcome truths" during his sermon in Chapter 9—truths that do not exist to entertain as much as to in-form and instruct. In an introduction to an edition of selected poems of Melville, poet Robert Penn Warren (1905–1989) writes: "Only by pressure and in pain is man 'routed' into a knowledge of his fate, and into whatever triumph, however limited and qualified, is possible in it."[14] T.S. Eliot (1888–1965) maintains that reading poetry should be "not merely an experience, but a serious experience."[15] To borrow a phrase from his poem "The Love Song of J. Alfred Prufrock," Eliot suggests that poetry should lead us to "overwhelming questions" about ourselves—questions that, ethically, we may be compelled to address and suffer in ways that may allow us revelations of more meaningful existences.

Moby-Dick is thus both meaningful and valuable to readers if they allow it to work itself upon their own prejudices and biases and ignorances and bigotries against others. Melville moves quickly to the practical and painful issue of exposing how and why humans are inclined to hatred of others instead of love of others—how, despite our knowledge of the good, humans more often than not do the opposite out of blind prejudice to conventional wisdoms and pieties. More to the point, virtually all the "unwelcome truths" Ishmael experiences in his tale challenge his long-learned and habitual *resistance* to embracing the diversity of the other.

---

[14] *Selected Poems of Herman Melville*, ed. Robert Penn Warren (Boston: David R. Godine, 2004) 69.

[15] See Karsten Harries, "Metaphor and Transcendence" in *On Metaphor*, ed. Sheldon Sacks (Chicago: University of Chicago Press, 1979) 86.

Take, for example, Ishmael suffering both the ignorance and knowledge of his own prejudices. What does it mean to be prejudiced? It means to prejudge things, which means to lack knowledge of opposite points of view; it means to be ignorant of the *other* and to blindly, even willfully act upon that ignorance. The ethical solution is for one to be compelled to recognize humanity's natural predispositions toward ignorances that may appear happily blissful. In addition, ethics compels one to understand that the best one can sometimes do is to recognize all sides of a given issue—especially its opposite sides—before choosing, then acting, then being fully responsible for both choice and act. To judge well and without prejudice means to weigh both sides fairly and act upon the fair balance. If one's knowledge of opposites of any situation exists, there is less chance of prejudice because there is more chance to sympathize with opposing points of view.

Perhaps because of a remarkably intact and healthy ego, Ishmael may be one of the finest examples in literature of a prejudiced human being attempting to reform himself. He suffers from the outset the American and materialistic tendency to believe only what he physically sees, and to base his belief on conventional instead of essential wisdom. What he both painfully and humorously comes to understand is this: what humans generally don't see affects their ethical beings more than what they do see, and that inward vision does not require external lighting to see its way; oftentimes, in fact, external light only hinders or impedes the path toward truth, for such light not only casts shadows in which truths may hide, but also light may shine on objects that deceptively appear to be truths. In Chapter 11, entitled "Nightgown," Ishmael arrives at this Pauline conclusion of personal identity, stating that "no man can ever feel his own identity aright except his eyes be closed; as if darkness were indeed the proper element of our essences, though light be more congenial to our clayey part." What does Paul say? "Look not at the things which are seen, but at the things which are not seen: for the things which are seen are temporal; but the things which are not seen are eternal."[16]

Ishmael physically sees something that looks like hell, only to discover that it is an African-American church. Ishmael physically looks upon Queequeg and sees a devil, only to discover soon afterwards that the cannibal becomes and forever will be the truest friend he may have. And although his prejudices begin to melt, they are bred deep in the bone, and readers witness Ishmael working time and again to resist his prejudices. Consider Ishmael's first overt claim of open-mindedness of Queequeg's tattooing: "It's only his outside," he says, "a man can be honest in any sort of skin" (Chap. 3). What is important here is Ishmael's ethical tone; it aspires *toward* self-assurance (as though he speaks in a way that he believes he *should* be thinking), for his prejudices continue to abide like so many prejudices that grow, callous-like, by pressures of habit to desensitize compassions. Or consider how Ishmael, in Chapter 4, is ashamed by how he thinks and acts toward his bedfellow. He notes that Queequeg "treated me with so much civility and consideration, while I was guilty of great rudeness; staring at him from the bed, and watching all his toilette motions; for the time my curiosity getting the better of my breeding."

Queequeg thus becomes essential to Ishmael's ethical upbuilding, for Queequeg unconsciously and continually offers the abrasive ethical offense, the unwelcome truth, and thereby the corrective to Ishmael's wide and varied prejudices.

---

[16] 2 Corinthians 4:18.

Three: Bosom friends and offended critics

Then there is Ishmael's utterly beautiful, funny, priceless line in Chapter 3: "Better sleep with a sober cannibal than a drunken Christian." How Ishmael draws that conclusion is compelling here, for his thoughts immediately prior to making that statement are saturated by his own conventional and pietistic prejudices—prejudices that he nonetheless is slowly and painfully unlearning. Ishmael describes the scene of getting into bed to sleep with Queequeg this way:

> "You gettee in," he [Queequeg] added, motioning to me with his tomahawk, and throwing the clothes to one side. He really did this in not only a civil but a really kind and charitable way. I stood looking at him for a moment. For all his tattooings he was on the whole a clean, comely looking cannibal. What's all this fuss I have been making about, thought I to myself—the man's a human being just as I am: he has as just as much reason to fear me, as I have to be afraid of him. Better sleep with a sober cannibal than a drunken Christian. (Chap. 3)

Here is Ishmael still looking at Queequeg from prejudiced western eyes instead of unprejudiced human eyes. Note also how this phrase that aspires to a cultural truism and battle cry in this book—"Better sleep with a sober cannibal than a drunken Christian"—has more of an advisory tone than a tone of a well-tested theory. Ishmael's formulation, in other words, suggests that it is the ethicist in him indicating a right course of action for him to take in the future instead of implying that he already has followed such a course of action in the past and is merely offering a maxim.

Nothing, however, prepares the conventional pietistic audience for the sudden rip tide away from shore and drop off into 70,000 fathoms of salt-water seas when Ishmael introduces the metaphor of marriage to portray his relationship with his cannibal-pagan-idolater friend. Moreover, nothing prepares the pietist for the ultimate dive into the deepest end of conventional Christian piety when Ishmael voluntarily turns pagan-idolater.

After he spends a night with Queequeg, Ishmael is a changed man—a transformed man—and the engulfing marriage metaphor that was only a mere drop of water at the beginning of Chapter 4 proves a flood that threatens conventional Christian pietism in the "Bosom Friend" episode (Chap. 10).

How did Melville suck the reader into the vortex of this most uncomfortable ethical position? And how are readers to respond to their "good Christian" narrator's potential homosexual or bisexual relationship with a pagan cannibal a mere 10 chapters into what arguably may be called The Great American Novel (which ostensibly involves a group of men sharing closing lodgings on a small whaler for upwards of three years to hunt a great white sperm whale called Moby Dick)? As for Ishmael turning idolater by joining Queequeg in his worship of the wooden idol Yojo: how are we to respond to the argument made by Ishmael (described in the next paragraph) that fails on logical grounds to fully reconcile the two love commandments with each other, yet nonetheless comforts Ishmael's Christian conscience? Did Melville really think readers would simply accept the abrasive ethical offenses he created against both conventional Christian morality and the Christian understanding of the sanctity of the first love commandment?

This is what the "Bosom Friend" episode reveals: After supper, Queequeg gives half of his money to Ishmael, then begins his prayer ritual. Ishmael momentarily considers if he would join in such idolatry if Queequeg were to offer the invitation. Before resolving his quandary affirmatively, Ishmael considers himself having been born and bred a good Christian. He also believes (presumably ignoring the first commandment) that God couldn't possibly be so jealous of such an insignificant wooden idol before developing his most effective argument, namely: that worship is to do the will of God, that the will of God is to do unto others as others would do to you, and that since Queequeg had united with Ishmael at the chapel, then Ishmael should willingly unite with Queequeg in idol worship—which he does before going to bed and talking late into the night with Queequeg.

Here again, Queequeg serves as a corrective for Ishmael by indirectly showing Ishmael's provincial limitations. Ishmael is not offended by Queequeg's unwitting imposition, for he embraces the corrective as he embraces Queequeg as a bosom friend and Queequeg's pagan worship as a viable act by which to carry out God's will. "No more my splintered heart and maddened hand were turned against the wolfish world. This soothing savage had redeemed it.... I'll try a pagan friend, thought I, since Christian kindness has proved but hollow courtesy" (Chap. 10). At the least, Ishmael understands in himself what an old man on the Isle of Serenia in Herman Melville's novel, *Mardi*, understands about the distinction between false and true piety: "He who hourly prays to Alma [Serenia's God], but lives not up to world-wide love and charity—that man is more an unbeliever than he who verbally rejects the Master, but does his bidding. Our lives are our Amens."[17] ("Essential passion is its own guarantee that there is something sacred," Kierkegaard as Christian apologist and

[17] Herman Melville, *Mardi and the Voyage Hither*, Chap. 187 (vol. 3 of the Northwestern-Newberry edition of *The Writings of Herman Melville* (Chicago: Northwestern University Press, 1970)).

critic of Christendom writes, as if commenting directly on the case of Queequeg and the old man on the Isle of Serenia: "When passion is essentially present in the pagan, even his idolatry is not devoid of devoutness."[18])

In the end, Ishmael appears to understand that the first love commandment is more subjectively or inwardly oriented while the second love commandment is more objectively or outwardly oriented. In other words, the first commandment may be followed by the inwardness of personal faith and belief without the showing of outward example, while the second commandment may be followed by outward action toward the neighbor, even as that outward action *appears* an affront to the first love commandment. Such reasoning, at least, is compatible with Ishmael's Pauline suggestions that physically seeing something as it merely appears to be is not tantamount to believing it.

And yet I, personally, still find myself not entirely comfortable with this conclusion.—But then I wonder if static *comfort* in a belief is the goal, for, as Kierkegaard claims, "faith

---

18 *Two Ages*, 64 (VIII 61). Elsewhere, one of Kierkegaard's pseudonyms takes up the cause and sympathizes with the authenticity that the passion for ethical practice and religious devotion brings to a human being, even if that human being does not consider him- or herself a Christian: "If someone who lives in the midst of Christianity enters, with knowledge of the true idea of God, the house of God, the house of the true God, and prays, but prays in untruth, and if someone lives in an idolatrous land but prays with all the passion of infinity, although his eyes are resting upon the image of an idol—where, then, is there more truth? The one prays in truth to God although he is worshiping an idol, the other prays in untruth to the true God and is therefore in truth worshiping an idol" (Søren Kierkegaard, *Concluding Unscientific Postscript to* Philosophical Fragments, 2 vols., eds. and trs. Howard V. Hong and Edna H. Hong (Princeton: Princeton University Press, 1992) 1:201 (VII 168).

is a restless thing."[19] Then I run across a passage like the following one, in which Ishmael speaks about being in bed with Queequeg and feeling cold:

> We felt very nice and snug, the more so since it was so chilly out of doors; indeed out of bed-clothes too, seeing that there was no fire in the room. The more so, I say, because truly to enjoy bodily warmth, some small part of you must be cold, for there is no quality in this world that is not what it is merely by contrast. Nothing exists in itself. If you flatter yourself that you are all over comfortable, and have been so a long time, then you cannot be said to be comfortable anymore. (Chap. 11)

In passages such as this, Melville once again trims the reader's sails and rights the reader's self, for there *is* no quality in this world that is not what it is except by contrast, and indeed nothing exists in itself, and if the reader were to exclude or in any other way deny the existence of the other, the reader would in fact be diminishing him- or herself.

Melville thus constructs his narrative so that even the most traditional or conservative reader may *at least once* have to question his or her conventional pietism before repressing, dismissing, ignoring, or outright rejecting the thought of, for instance, a potentially gay or bisexual idolater at the helm of The Great American Novel.

That said, Ishmael endorses conventional Christian wisdom when he can. He critiques the bar of the Spouter Inn, for instance, with temperance society language in Chapter 3 to appeal to teetotalling readers and to present himself as "one of

---

[19] Søren Kierkegaard, *For Self-Examination and Judge for Yourself!* Ed. trans. Howard V. Hong and Edna H. Hong (Princeton: Princeton University Press, 1998) 17 (XII 308.

them." Then he bathes readers in a beautiful and clear baptismal fount of traditional Christian orthodoxy in "The Chapel," "The Pulpit," and "The Sermon" episodes in Chapters 7-9, all of which at least convince some readers that his more traditional Christian affinities are genuine. Then he calls himself a "good Christian" in Chapter 10, "born and bred in the bosom of the infallible Presbyterian Church" (despite that the adjective "infallible" might betray an ironic tone toward the Church).

Ishmael, in effect, works from the inside out. He is a Christian insider. But he also wants us to call him Ishmael, which implies from the outset that he has some halibut-sized bone to pick about his status as outcast, and that the bone to pick may not so much be with God as it is with what Ishmael calls "civilized hypocrisies and bland deceits" of a brand of "Christian kindness [that has] proved but hollow courtesy" (Chap. 10), courtesy that mocks any sense of "infallibility" on the Church's part. In the "Bosom Friend" episode, Melville fires in earnest his shot across his readers' bows in a daring attempt to illuminate how a pietistic reader's conventional wisdoms regarding sexuality and worship *really* "weigh…in the scales of the New Testament" (Chap. 1). Even Melville's own American publisher and friend angrily stated in a review of *Moby-Dick* that Ishmael's kneeling in comradeship with Queequeg before the black idol, Yojo, "violated the most sacred associations of life."[20]

How Ishmael describes Queequeg and his relationship also perhaps offended Melville's publisher and friend. The description of Queequeg as "George Washington cannibalistically developed" (Chap. 10) may strike uncomfortably bold

[20] Howard Vincent, *The Trying-Out of* Moby-Dick (Carbondale, Illinois: Southern Illinois University Press, 1949) 80.

chords for many readers when coupled with Queequeg's potentially homosexual relationship with Ishmael: George Washington, Father of the modern American tribe, compared to Queequeg, some savage from some island that isn't even "down on any map" (Chap. 12) and about as far from George Washington's literal and cultural birthplace as a body can travel without having to come back. The fact that, at the end of Chapter 9, readers see Father Mapple alone before his God, his pulpit, and his Bible, and then at the beginning of Chapter 10, readers see Queequeg alone before his idol, his stove hearth, and a large book that he cannot read nor understand suggests the potentially uncomfortable possibility that Melville also sees little difference between the good Christian Father Mapple and the pagan cannibal who, after all, will be seen later lacking Christian papers while looking for a harpooneer's job on the Christian-owned *Pequod.* Or consider Melville critiquing "good Christian" financiers when the author has Queequeg give half of all his money—thirty dollars in silver—to Ishmael: thirty pieces of silver used not for paying off an act of betrayal but for a love that brokers nothing less than infinite indebtedness to the other.

Then, consider how Ishmael describes Queequeg's good and simple soul in the "Bosom Friend" episode:

> Savage though he was, and hideously marred about the face—at least to my taste—his countenance yet had a something in it which was by no means disagreeable. You cannot hide the soul. Through all his unearthly tattooings, I thought I saw traces of a simple honest heart; and in his large, deep eyes, fiery black and bold, there seemed tokens of a spirit that would dare a thousand devils. And besides all this, there was a certain lofty bearing about the Pagan, which even his uncouthness could not altogether maim.

> He looked like a man who had never cringed and never had had a creditor.... [He was] content with his own companionship; always equal to himself. Surely this was a touch of fine philosophy; though no doubt he had never heard there was such a thing as that.... He seemed to take to me quite as naturally and unbiddenly as I to him; and when our smoke was over, he pressed his forehead against mine, clasped me around the waist, and said that henceforth we were married; meaning, in his country's phrase, that we were bosom friends; he would gladly die for me, if need should be. (Chap. 10)

It's beautiful. It's touching. It's delicate. It's sweet. It's innocent. It's a truly healthy marriage of a Christian and a pagan, of Christianity and the other.

Four: "Ambiguity is richness"

For better or for worse, the bedroom has become both a political and a religious issue in the contemporary world, and Melville anticipated it. Knowing that Melville constantly challenged the religious, ethical, and social conventions of his times throughout his entire literary career, the issue of bisexuality or homosexuality is invoked in *Moby-Dick* to challenge the past and present prevailing winds of Christian heterosexual monogamy.

The issue has direct bearing on how humans love or do not love neighbors based upon sexual orientation or, in the particular case of Ishmael and Queequeg, our mere *presumption* of the thought of their sexual orientations. The issue also is invariably brought up by high school- or college-aged students who read *Moby-Dick*, most if not all of whom want to know if Ishmael and Queequeg are gay. As instructor/facilitator of such classroom discussions, I remind students that, lest they fall into the trap of prejudice about which Ishmael has been warning us since Chapter 1, they had better have airtight evidence that speaks to whatever opinion they hold. In other words, opinions about ways of life based upon prejudgments or presumptions can be risky. It can even make us look as comical as the Nantucket Captain Peleg in Chapter 16, who is "full of…insular prejudices, and rather distrustful of all aliens, unless they hailed from Cape Cod or [Martha's] Vineyard" (Cape Cod and Martha's Vineyard are the two nearest land masses to Nantucket, approximately 15 miles away to the north and the west).

I then note to students that issues of bisexuality and homosexuality have never been alien to or uncommon in any human culture, especially in cases where members of a single-gendered population are alone together for extended periods of time, say, on two- or three-year whaling cruises. Despite that the morally ambiguous "Don't ask, don't tell" rule gained much press some years ago with the issue of gay people serving in the military, the rule has no doubt existed unspoken since the beginning of human history. Given such history, and given many Melville scholars' researched opinions that address Melville's own alleged bisexual orientation, it is a wonder that Melville's text does not take a more overt position regarding whether or not a sexual relationship exists between Ishmael and Queequeg. His choice to remain ambiguous on this and other like issues, however, is understandable—and for good reasons.

The obvious, although perhaps not primary, reason for maintaining ambiguity is that Melville's book would have been immediately panned by conventional mid-19th century critics if Melville developed the Ishmael-Queequeg relationship as overtly homosexual. Melville is also shrewd enough to know that tabloid-style shock has a short half-life when it comes to educating, informing, and transforming the minds and hearts of readers on controversial topics, and that intentional ambiguity goes much further to compel readers not so much to wonder outwardly about Ishmael and Queequeg's sexuality as to suffer inwardly the *license* to wonder about Ishmael and Queequeg's sexuality. It is as if Melville challenges the reader to make a judgment on flimsy evidence of bisexual or homosexual orientation so as to have a reader suffer the feelings related to prejudice, bias, and bigotry that such a judgment necessarily would stir. Interestingly, such prejudice equally applies to the reader who believes only that the Ishmael-Queequeg relationship is nonsexual and platonic. For, if one concludes the relationship is either sexual *or* only platonic, the conclusion can only be based on unsubstantiated presentiment. There is neither clear nor factual evidence either way. We prejudice ourselves simply by siding with one view or the other instead of plodding through the murky quagmire of the ambiguous unknown.

What Ishmael says in Chapter 85 about the nature of the part-watery/part-airy substance that is blown out of a whale's spout applies here: "My dear sir," he writes, "in this world it is not so easy to settle these plain things. I have ever found your plain things the knottiest of all." Although Ishmael provides the reader a unique view into his and Queequeg's lodgings, there are personal and private moments between individuals, Melville the earnest and complex moralist seems to suggest, that ought to be no one else's business but their own, for individuals lacking private or interior lives are not complete individuals. Subsequently, Melville suggests that Ishmael and Queequeg's private relationship ought to be respected as private.

But why do we remain voyeuristically interested in it? Why do we want to pry into what is clearly a private and consensual act? Why should we care? Why do we seek to validate or condemn private events that we may have no right to validate or condemn? More specifically, how does all this weigh in the scales of the New Testament, of love of the other, of love of the spirit, of *agape*? Just as Ishmael feels "guilty of great rudeness" when he finds himself "staring at [Queequeg] from the bed, and watching all his toilette motions" in Chapter 4, so Melville perhaps wants us to feel guilty of great rudeness by voyeuristically peaking into Ishmael and Queequeg's private rooms, and prejudging their most extraordinary love and friendship on the basis of distracting circumstantial evidence that is sexual in nature.

Another reason Melville may have been intentionally ambiguous on this and like issues addresses a literary and quasi-theological concern: Any great artist will be ambiguous on key issues, because, as Argentinean writer Jorge Luis Borges notes, "Ambiguity is richness."[21] Leave public facts to newspaper reporters and half-truths to propagandists and lobbyists and partisans; art floats on elemental truths that are not so easily cornered and objectified in public pronouncements but, at best, suggested, hinted upon, and evoked in the shadows of language and underneath the bleachers of public arenas of discourse. In other words, art shows, not tells. The truth art offers thus comes to us more powerfully by indirect means and through our own capacity for knowing and believing. To borrow a line from Bob Dylan, art "knows too much to argue or to judge."[22] Some suggestions or hints or evocations may be more compelling or provocative than others,

[21] Jorge Luis Borges, *Ficciones* (New York: Grove Press, 1962) 52 (fr. "Pierre Menard, Author of the *Quixote*").

[22] Bob Dylan, *Lyrics 1962-2001* (New York: Simon and Schuster, 2004) (fr. "Love Minus Zero/No Limits").

but art exists in great part to suggest that there are as many and diverse ways to interpret truth as their are people to interpret the truth, because truth in this context is more inward than outward, more subjective than objective. Truth would not be richly meaningful if it was merely and objectively black-and-white, an interstate highway system with no choice of exit ramps, entrance ramps, and blue highways. Art (and how we perceive truth in art) can't be seen directly, but only through a glass darkly.[23]

Yet a deeper reason for Melville's use of ambiguity on both the issues of sexuality and of religion becomes clearer if readers remind themselves that, in part, *Moby-Dick* may be said to portray the mending of outcast hearts and selves that are separated from each other. A fully loving, compassionate, and whole self requires more than blindly siding with or being blindsided by conventional wisdom or of choosing one side of a coin and prejudicially affirming its existence to the exclusion of the existence of the other side of the coin of which we choose to remain ignorant. Melville is thus intent upon driving the nature of choice based upon prejudice into a corner and routing it out, and to do this he constructs instances in which Ishmael and his readers are tempted to judge and choose thoughts, words, and deeds that (without true examination) yield nothing more than a bigoted reaction based upon prejudicial thinking.

Many of these important "shore" chapters of *Moby-Dick* thus call upon readers to bend and lean toward the other, to not deny the other lest readers deny themselves—unlike the captain who takes center stage for the rest of the novel and acts in such a way as to confess to his first mate near the end: "'Aye aye Starbuck, 'tis sweet to lean sometimes...and would

[23] See I Corinthians 13:12.

old Ahab had leaned oftener than he has'" (Chap. 134.) In many cases, examples in these opening chapters accomplish this by way of compelling readers to feel what it is like to be the other, to be the stranger, the alien—or, as the cliché goes, to walk a mile in someone else's shoes before judging that other person.

One other particularly pathos-filled and humorous instance of prejudgment is noteworthy. It is in "The Ramadan" episode (Chap. 17), which begins with Ishmael respecting Queequeg's religious ritual of fasting. He claims with an air of mock diplomacy that he has "the greatest respect towards everybody's religious obligations, never mind how comical," for Ishmael cannot "find it in [his] heart to undervalue even a congregation of ants worshipping a toad-stool." He then maintains that "we good Presbyterians should be charitable in these things, and not fancy ourselves so vastly superior to other mortals, pagans or what not, because of their half-crazy conceits on these subjects." Here, Ishmael (now with a self-satirizing sense of his own innate self-righteousness) is fully respecting the neighbor, whoever that neighbor is. Despite this tacitly "moral" embrace of the other, however, Ishmael quickly is offended by how Queequeg's private religious service causes such a panicked ruckus among himself, the chamber-maid, and the proprietor, Mrs. Hussey—all of whom jump to the conclusion that Queequeg has committed suicide behind locked doors. The door to Ishmael and Queequeg's room is finally broken down by Ishmael, against Mrs. Hussey's admonitions, and Ishmael is left angered and embarrassed by his own over-reaction. He brusquely takes his anger out on Queequeg, for, according to Ishmael, "it seemed so downright senseless and insane to be sitting there all day and half the night on [Queequeg's] hams in a cold room, holding a piece of wood on his head." When Queequeg's silent fasting ends the next morning, Ishmael is intent upon arguing that "all these Lents, Ramadans, and prolonged ham-squattings in cold, cheerless rooms were stark nonsense; bad for the health; useless for the soul; opposed, in short, to the obvious laws of Hygiene and common sense." He concludes by claiming that "hell is an idea first borne on an undigested apple-dumpling; and since then perpetuated through the hereditary dyspepsias nurtured by Ramadans." After Queequeg tells a story of the only time he recalls suffering from dyspepsia, namely, by eating too much human flesh one day, the episode concludes with these reflections by Ishmael:

> After all, I do not think that my remarks about religion made much impression upon Queequeg. Because, in the first place, he somehow seemed dull of hearing on that important subject, unless considered from his own point of view; and, in the second place, he did not more than one third understand me, couch my ideas simply as I would; and, finally, he no doubt thought he knew a good deal more about the true religion than I did. He looked at me with a sort of condescending concern and compassion, as though he thought it a great pity that such a sensible young man should be so hopelessly lost to evangelical pagan piety.
>
> At last we rose and dressed; and Queequeg, taking a prodigiously hearty breakfast of chowders of all sorts, so that the landlady should not make much profit by reason of his Ramadan, we sallied out to board the Pequod, sauntering along, and picking our teeth with halibut bones.

In the contexts of human prejudice and a "Christian" embrace of diversity, this comical episode addresses how humans ought to suffer to accept not only religious rituals other than their own, but also recognize the "absurdity" of their own religious rituals, their own lents, no matter how far beyond common reason they extend. Plentifully laced with humor, the episode recognizes the fundamental *likeness* among all religious practices, namely, that belief and faith is true only if its restless borders transgress and pass beyond human understanding, for the infinite cannot be adequately expressed nor contained within any unambiguous manmade system of logic.

What makes this episode particularly humorous, perhaps even more humorous than Ishmael's perception of Queequeg's religious activities, is Ishmael's own anguished vacillation between extending religious compassion and taking religious offense. (This is somewhat analogous to Mrs. Hussy's vacillation between her compassionate maternal worries over the potential reaction of Queequeg's mother and sister to sad news of Queequeg's possible suicide and, conversely, her offended pragmatic concerns over maintaining the good name of her business establishment despite such a death). Comic resolution is achieved only by Ishmael and Queequeg sharing a hearty breakfast and, afterwards, picking their teeth together with halibut bones—in a phrase, the courage to accept acceptance of the other. Taken all in all, the episode celebrates how intimately the earnestly sublime idea of religion coexists with the comically absurd. In other words, just as Queequeg's notions about Yojo and his Ramadan may be considered "most absurd" by Ishmael, so too could the Christian belief in the paradoxical notion of God-turned-man or body-turned-bread or blood-turned-wine be considered absurd by non-Christians.

Such "absurdities" on which the stuff of miracle is made does not cancel out the subjective truth they may have for the individual believer—in fact, the absurd enhances the sublimity. God can't exist for humans as omnipotent and humans can't exist with God's gift of free will to humans without a concept of the absurd, for it is precisely the absurd that passes beyond human understanding. Humans' powerful weapons of reason and speculation, in other words, do not contain the true essence of faith because they cannot contain the true essence of faith. Either human reason attempts to defy faith by making faith appear reasonable or man's reason utterly surrenders to faith. That said—and at the risk of sounding reasonable—one aspect of becoming fully human (which is at least as old as Socrates) means to be able to discriminate between that which is in the realm of objective reason and knowledge and that which is in the realm of subjective faith. And it is precisely at this point of discrimination where humor leaves us standing naked on our own shores, for when we laugh at the odd coupling of odd things, we confess to a great truth about the radical limitations of the intellect and its essential inferiority to those subjective capacities of the heart, capacities like love, faith, hope, and belief. A disarming, accepting laughter may be what Ishmael evokes in his readers when, after all tension in him between compassion and offense finally breaks, he finds himself sauntering along and picking his teeth with his good neighbor and friend, while they both unwittingly move toward boarding an ill-fated deck on which high tragedy plays out.

3

The Self-Deceiver in Henrik Ibsen's *Peer Gynt*[1]

One: To be or to become, that is the question

Emblazoned atop the proscenium at Denmark's Royal Copenhagen Theater (at least during the early to mid-19th century) was the motto, "Not for entertainment only."[2] Despite its Calvinist gloss, it's a fair motto for a theater, encouraging the audience to recognize good theatrical art not simply as "art for art's sake," but rather as art that is capable of addressing ethical, philosophical, and religious issues, or as art that offers hints about who or what or why we are. Such art serves as crucial messages in a bottle, washed up along the shores of time and human existence for us to read—clues that help readers and viewers attend especially to human existence. How readers and viewers act upon such messages in such bottles of course helps determine most how their lives are ultimately played out—because, as Ibsen comes to know along with the likes of Kierkegaard, free will is an essential key to becoming fully human. We have free will to run our life amok or earnestly navigate through life's muck. But first, according to Kierkegaard and Ibsen, we must know what it means to be a human self and the likes of Peer Gynt helps us understand

---

[1] Henrik Ibsen, *Peer Gynt*, tr. Rolf Fjelde (Minneapolis: University of Minnesota Press, 1980). Page numbers will be cited following quoted passages.

[2] *Repetition*, 155, 366 (Notes).

what it means to become a human, what it means to have a self and to be a self. According to the Kierkegaard passage that introduces the foreword to the Fjelde edition of *Peer Gynt*, to have a self and to be a self is "the greatest concession, an infinite concession, given to man, but it is also eternity's claim upon him"[3]—that is, to have and to be a self—to forge such a self—is both infinite gift and ethical task.

•

Ibsen's Peer Gynt ranks as a central archetypal figure in world literature. Just as Plato gives us Socrates, Chaucer and Dante give us themselves as travelers along stages on life's way, Cervantes gives us Don Quixote, Goethe gives us Faust, so Ibsen gives us Peer Gynt. Each epic character is an "Everyman" insofar as their authors have managed to construct them in such a way as to make them efficiently and compactly mirror who parts of us are and, on an ethical plane, point to who we may or may not want to be or become.

Heroes may be considered models of which readers may become if readers follow their ethical leads; anti-heroes may be considered models of who readers are and who readers may not want to continue to be. As an all-too-human protagonist, the double-minded, double-visioned Peer Gynt who lives a duplicitous life may suggest who readers more often than not *are*; his thoughts and actions expose the follies and foibles of us foolish mortals, allowing Ibsen as satirist to help his readers see themselves in such a singular way as to attend ethically to improve themselves and their lot. For there inevitably is something of a double-minded Peer Gynt in all human beings; and Ibsen, by putting a mirror up to human nature as

---

[3] *Peer Gynt*, ix. I have used the Hong translation from *The Sickness Unto Death*, 21 (XI 135).

human nature so often *is*, *indirectly* points to who we may *become* in the best sense of the word.

But deliberately choosing who we may become requires disclosure of possibilities, and by showing who we may be allows us at least the understanding (if not yet the will) to reject patterns of behaviors, habits and beliefs if we can see flaws in such behaviors, habits, and beliefs. It is ultimately the ethical question of "how" we are that best determines who we may become, for "how" we live our lives presupposes choice. In the case of *Peer Gynt*, *how* we appropriate the message of the Peer Gynt in us may help us determine *who* or *what* we may become, which makes *Peer Gynt* transformative literature.

The process of becoming fully human in an ethical sense, then, must not stop with insane Ophelia's reigned words in *Hamlet* when she utters: "Lord, we know what we are but know not what we may be" (4.5.48–49). Becoming fully human requires *understanding* who we are (double-minded, indifferent, noncommittal), then *imagining* what we ethically may become (deliberate), then choosing, then striving to become that which we currently are not, all of which is the sometimes painful work involving long periods of self-examination and psychological gestation.

In his book *The Sickness Unto Death*, Kierkegaard considers that the vast majority of us duplicitous humans don't even know we are in despair because we haven't fully figured out that we have a far more singular and integrated self to which we can relate ourselves (made all-the-more difficult in a digital age in which continuous partial attention rules the day).[4] How one comes to know who one is and how one comes to know who one may become subsequently requires a psychological stripping away of layers of who one *thinks* one is

[4] See pp. 50-51.

or who one thinks one *appears* to be. Figuratively speaking, such a process is a shedding of one's false or apparent selves to get to the essential self. Such self-examination requires a peeling away of one's deceptions and self-deceptions, a call to rendering all appearances as nothing for the sake of human honesty (which, according to Kierkegaard, is neither too lenient nor too stringent[5]); it is, in other words, a terribly humbling call to shed an ego in which an individual invests heavily throughout his or her life.

The onion scene in Act 5 of *Peer Gynt* suggests the beginning of Peer's more or less deliberate examination of himself, a stripping himself of himself. Peer finds himself peeling an onion, examining each layer, and likening each layer to a deceptive or self-deceptive part of his life. This is self-examination at its most fundamental. In a larger sense, the onion scene is a metaphor for the play as a whole, for the whole play examines how prevalent deceit and self-deceit is to the human condition and, by indirection, how essential what Kierkegaard calls human honesty is to human beings.

Peer Gynt is from beginning to end a story of a journey to find one's self, to understand oneself, and to consciously will to become that self transparently; Peer Gynt, however, not only journeys in his own highly imaginative-escapist mind, but he also journeys throughout the world and throughout his life. He always thinks that he is true to himself and, if we consider his ordinary "self" as being a lying, self-deceiving self as his mother describes Peer in the opening lines of the play, then he is indeed always true to himself, for he is always lying (or *almost* always lying) to himself. But we would be deceiving

---

[5] Søren Kierkegaard, *The Moment and Late Writings*, eds. and trs. Howard V. Hong and Edna H. Hong (Princeton: Princeton University Press, 1998) 46 (XIV 52).

ourselves (or at least contradicting ourselves) if we ever were to consider a false self to be a true self, so we must conclude that Peer is often (but not *always*) lost to his truer self. The extent to which Ibsen considers a person being lost as elemental—even essential—to the human condition is something each of us may judge for ourselves. Henry David Thoreau writes: "Not till we are lost, in other words, not till we have lost the world, do we begin to find ourselves, and realize where we are and the infinite extent of our relations"[6]—which is a passage that may lend some sympathy and meaning to Peer's (and our) many wanderings.

Two: To be oneself enough versus to choose oneself

Ibsen's play *Peer Gynt* wasn't meant to be performed, but rather read as a philosophical prose poem. It has a companion prose poem that also looks like a play, entitled *Brand*, the main character being a minister on a radical mission from God and serves as counterpoint to Peer Gynt. A primary philosophical source for both plays is rooted in Kierkegaard's two-volume *Either/Or*.

Volume One of *Either/Or* focuses upon the ever-shifting, ever-noncommittal personality of what Kierkegaard dubs the esthetic individual, namely, one who lives most immediately by his esthetic senses alone; one who, like Peer Gynt, prefers to address issues in his life by, in Ibsen's terms, "going roundabout" instead of going "straight through" (see, e.g., 207) to the heart of problems and of life. The esthete is a seducer of many, but never commits to anyone or anything. The esthete is like Peer insofar as his ever-duplicitous double-mindedness has slit his vision of the world in two. He cannot commit to anything because he cannot decide upon anything for certain. He risks

[6] *Walden and Other Writings*, 232 (fr. "The Village" in *Walden*).

nothing, thus his life becomes meaningless because he values nothing enough to take any risks at all. He is anchorless and rudderless, floating as it were on the shoals of a shallow existence. He doesn't even live in the present because he lacks any substantive concept of a past or a future.

Volume Two of Kierkegaard's *Either/Or*—the "Or" of the title—represents the ethical and ethical-religious individual in the persona of a sermonizing judge and married man named William, who esteems ideas of commitment, duty, deliberation, choice, patience, hope, love of neighbor, and love of God—themes represented in *Peer Gynt* particularly by Solveig and in Ibsen's *Brand* by the minister Brand himself.

•

This is how things stand with Peer up through Act 3:

In Act 1, Peer is a young man with a dangerously illusive sense of unbridled freedom and carelessness. He doesn't concern himself about his heritage, his mother, a bride whom he snatches from a groom at the altar, the ethics of his culture, and even the compassionate and devoted heart of Solveig, the girl who loves him. To quote from Kierkegaard's esthetic pseudonym A, "he was a man that was to himself enough"[7] long before he enters the gates of the troll kingdom in Act 2 and its huge estate built upon compromise in the worst sense of that term—gates which even the Troll King himself tells Peer that "Here it's easy to enter in,/But the gate isn't made to swing out again" (60).

By Act 2, Peer's nightmarish life is in full swing. Meanwhile, a few half-baked decisions and tumbles in the hay

---

[7] Søren Kierkegaard, *Either/Or* (2 vols.), eds. and trs. Howard V. Hong and Edna H. Hong (Princeton: Princeton University Press, 1998) 1:203 (I 178).

in the troll kingdom begin to rear multi-headed problems like the 300-headed grandmother of the trollish devil himself.

In Act 3, Peer, with his lack of will and commitment, is offended by witnessing a boy cutting off his finger to avoid military duty. Peer desperately seeks to bar himself from any thoughts that may lead him upon a much harder and narrower path toward becoming a truer self. In other words, Peer in Act 3 is only beginning to meet with evidence of eternity's demand upon the self—and he is scared to death. He begins running like a fugitive *from* himself. When asked where Peer is going at the end of Act 3, Peer says, "To the sea.... Yes; and farther still." The perhaps accidental pun on the word "sea" in the English translation is precious, for "seeing" (or more precisely "not seeing") is Peer's problem. His ambitious but vacuous life demands that he not be satisfied by plainly and simply seeing himself; instead, he leapfrogs over honest vision and seals the fate of his later years, for in Act 4 Peer is 25 years older but none the wiser.

Like Kierkegaard, then, Ibsen ponders the gravity of free will and choice in becoming human, exploring how ethical exercises of free will and choice inform the backdrop of eternity's demand upon each human self.

For the likes of trolls (animals in human garb), Ibsen might say that any freedom is a false freedom, bereft of responsibility or accountability, a sort of anarchy of the spirit in which one always escapes from oneself instead of ethically to oneself. This escape cheats oneself of even the great concession made to humankind, that is, of having any real choice at all in one's life. The troll stands prior to choice instead of amid the responsible task that free will demands; the troll's desire is for "both-and" (he wants it all), not the true either/or of life that positively asserts human existence by affirming mortal limitations and mitigating humans' self-aggrandizing desires to be godlike. This default "choice" (more like a drive or an inclination than a choice) toward gratification is immediate and physical, and thus ephemeral; pleasure, at its best, is hedonistic; self-satisfaction is met by meeting the status quo of existence only; the Troll motto is to be yourself enough instead of being true to yourself, as Socrates maintains, or choosing yourself, as Kierkegaard's Judge William maintains.[8]

To choose oneself is thus the opposite of human as Troll. Humans striving to become more complete humans through the gravity of choice embody possibilities for an ethical sense of direction, a commitment to a purpose or destiny that offers a deeper, more inward meaning to otherwise transitory and outward lives.

The secret of the life of the troll is not unlike how Kierkegaard describes the secret of speculative (Hegelian) philosophers. Their "secret in [their] comprehending," Kierkegaard writes, "is simply to sew without fastening the end and without knotting the thread, and this is why, wonder of wonders, [they] can go on sewing and sewing, that is, pulling the thread through." Kierkegaard concludes this thought by maintaining that the ethics of "Christianity, on the other hand, fastens the end by means of the paradox"[9]—a phrase in which Kierkegaard means that Christians knot the end of the thread of life at the *beginning* of a conscious life of faith and belief. This knot and sewing analogy applies to how Peer pitifully attempts to stitch a life together in Acts 2 and 3 without making any initial ethical movements (predicated on believing or having faith in something) that would make thereby hold the weave together.

---

[8] See, e.g., *Either/Or* 2:270 (II 242).

[9] *The Sickness Unto Death*, 93 (XI 204).

Three: "My kingdom—no, half if it—for a horse!"

By the time we see Peer Gynt some 20 years later in Act 4, it is as though he does not even need to run anymore to stay away from himself. It is as though he has so completely deceived himself that he can stand right next to himself and not even see himself. In this context, his life has not progressed but regressed. He has made a fortune in slave trading and the selling of pagan images in China, and his triumphant business acumen becomes what he calls his "moral code" (97). He is a proud and unscrupulous capitalist, materialist, and hedonist. If the maxim "Age and intelligence begets deceit and self-deceit" was ever an arguable assertion, the model of Peer Gynt would cancel any doubts of its veracity. The smarter and older and richer Peer has become, the less wise and more childish and more bereft of spirit he too has become.

Even more than the previous three acts, Act 4 is reminiscent of a passage from Fyodor Dostoevsky's *Notes From Underground*, a short novel that critics maintain was the turning point in Dostoevsky's career and one that preceded his mature works, most notably *Crime and Punishment* and *The Brothers Karamazov*. The first-person narrator of Dostoevsky's novel begins his story with the words, "I am a sick man…I am a wicked man. An unattractive man. I think my liver hurts. However, I don't know a fig about my sickness, and am not sure what it is that hurts me."[10] Unlike Peer, however, the Underground Man is passionately interested in examining himself and getting to the root of his sad existence. Later in his narrative, he offers this illumination, which is best placed in relief against Peer's lack of self-consciousness in Act 4:

[10] Fyodor Dostoevsky, *Notes From Underground*, trs. Richard Pevear and Larissa Volokhonsky (New York: Knopf, 1993) 3.

> In every man's memories there are such things as he will reveal not to everyone, but perhaps only to friends. There are also such as he will reveal not even to friends, but only to himself, and that in secret. Then, finally, there are such as a man is afraid to reveal even to himself, and every decent man will have accumulated quite a few things of this sort. That is, one might say: the more decent a man is, the more of them he will have.[11]

Peer Gynt has so skillfully mismanaged his life during his years away from his homeland, it is a wonder that he has not completely estranged his authentic self from himself. But humans are elastic and resilient, and as capable of the greatest feats of self-deception as they are of deep and profound contrition. If pride is ever to come before a fall, Peer, in what seems an unwitting mid-life crisis that doubles as a protracted adolescence, shows off his superb acts of deception and self-deception time and again in Act 4. There are a thousand secrets in his life and psyche that he has buried (along with honest sacrifices unmade and good deeds undone); it is no wonder he cannot see his way clear to a vision of a contrite heart burning for an intact self. He is not unlike the person in despair about whom Kierkegaard contrasts to a balloonist:

> Just as a balloonist ascends by throwing off weights, so the person in despair sinks by more and more determinedly throwing off all the good (for the weight of the good is elevating); he sinks, privately thinking, of course, that he is ascending—and he is indeed growing lighter.[12]

[11] *Notes From Underground*, 39 (in Part 1, Chap. 11).
[12] *The Sickness Unto Death*, 110.

It is not surprising, then, that the end of Act 4 takes place in an insane asylum, where its director, Prof. Begriffenfeldt, agrees with Peer Gynt when Peer claims that he is entirely himself in everything that he does—for when reason is dead, Begriffenfeldt notes,

> Everyone here is himself to the gills,
> Completely himself and nothing else—
> So far in himself he can't come back.
> Everyone's shut in his cask of skin;
> He dives in the self's fermenting murk,
> Hermetically sealed by a self-made cork—
> Shrinking his staves down a well of brine.
> No one has tears for the others' griefs,
> Or feels at all for the others' beliefs. (142)

In other words, Peer Gynt's radical lack of any concept of the *other* makes him, as Begriffenfeldt later says "Himself by being beside himself" (145).

What has contributed to Peer's decadence of self over the years? This is no simple question, for accountability may begin with the choices of Peer's father, to the choices of Peer's loving and enabling mother, to Peer's choices himself—his opting, for instance, for a fantasy life instead of a life built upon an imagination ethically grounded in the actual world; or his choosing to fear the type of action that requires faith in order to be genuinely courageous; or his double-minded flights of deception and self-deception, where troll-like and in the spirit of what witches say in Shakespeare's *Macbeth*, "fair is foul" and "foul is fair;"[13] where Bible verses are either misquoted or entirely made up to suit his whims; where he has

[13] *Macbeth*, 1.3.

compromised himself in the worst spirit of that word; and where he is "to himself enough" when, as he walks along desert wastelands, he compromises even Shakespeare's Richard the Third's valiant either/or: "My kingdom—no, half of it—for a horse!" (115); and in Act 4, he takes great pride in and defends the whole realm of his half-existence. It is no wonder that he was so offended by the young man of Act 3 who, in a radical choice of either/or, cuts off his finger to avoid military duty, especially if we accept Kierkegaard's definition of offense as being a state of "unhappy admiration." [14] "An irreplaceable finger," Peer cries out, "Lost!... / ...For all time, never to—/Yes, think it; wish it; *will* it so—/But to *do* it! No, I can't follow him there" (71).

The task of becoming fully human requires, according to Howard Hong, the ability "to live in that which one understands," in other words, to *do* what one *understands* to be the good. And when the likes of Peer has, through habit, kept himself from his real self for so long, the task seems virtually impossible. Act 4 offers many instances of Peer as a complete stranger to himself, farther from himself than the stars are from the earth.

Then comes Act 5.

Four: After stage lights fade

Act 5 opens with stage directions noting that it is sunset. Weather is stormy along the Norwegian coastline, where Peer, with trollish tail between his legs, is on board a ship homeward-bound. Twenty years have passed since the end of Act 4, his clothes are worn, he is weather-beaten, and his face appears harder. He is perhaps in his early 60s.

---

[14] *The Sickness Unto Death*, 86 (XI 197).

We need not read too far into the opening scene to know that Peer continues to seek desperate refuge *from* himself, for his narcissism is as strong as ever. He describes his conscience as a "downy pillow" (156). When the ship begins to sink, he fails miserably at lifeboat ethics, calling for someone to bring "all [his] baggage on deck!" (160) instead of calling all hands on deck for all to be aware of the danger to their lives.

Peer then meets the Strange Passenger. Is he an actual person? Or a figment of Peer's dwarfed ethical conscience defending its turf? Perhaps it doesn't matter, especially because Peer's sense of ethical reality is so porous. The Strange Passenger wants Peer's corpse after he dies so that he may be opened up and his selfishness be brought to light. He asks Peer if Peer has ever once in his life "Known the victory only dread can give" (164). By "dread" the Passenger suggests the kind of anxiety experienced by one committing to an honesty and self-honesty that compels an earnest human being into the arena of deliberation and choice toward good action. When the Strange Passenger is rebuked by Peer as being absurd, the Strange Passenger tells Peer not to worry about this current exchange, for "No one dies halfway through the last act" (165).

Peer of course survives the sinking ship, and on shore he comes within earshot of the eulogy of the man who, back in Act 3 and some 45 years ago, cut off his finger to avoid military duty. The eulogy praises the man's ability to be a humble servant the remainder of his life, especially to his children (despite that they turn out to be a thankless lot). Then, Peer, in yet another extraordinary act of self-deception, likens *his* life to the deliberate, committed, humble life of the dead man.

Then comes the famous onion scene in which Peer actually sees—by peeling layers away from an onion to its coreless middle and by comparing each peeling to each stage of his life—that his life has been merely that: a series of thinly veiled persona and facades without any core. He realizes that, time and time again, he has tricked and bamboozled himself and loused up his life. But even at this critical and contemplative self-examination, Peer fails to yield the fruit of a contrite heart, and he continues to escape from himself by simple denial: "To hell with brooding!" he declares (177).

Fortunately, nightmarish thoughts of anxious dread (like psychological ground troops commanded by the Strange Passenger) begin a major assault on his psyche, and he suffers claims made on his many thoughtless sins of omission: thoughts he should have thought, songs he should have sung, tears he should have wept, and deeds he should have done. (The scene perhaps is meant to remind readers that, despite how humans attempt to live without regret for the sake of forgetting the past, the concept of regret has powerful future-oriented therapeutic value toward the development of a contrite heart.)

Then comes the Button-molder—a sort of Dickensian ghost of Christmas Past, Present, and Future perhaps conjured up by Peer's repressed conscience of a fictional character whom Peer liked to role-play as a child (see 73). The Button-molder scenes move Peer to the play's end, but not to a clean and pat *dramatic* resolution within the confines of the play.

The Button-molder first diagnoses Peer. When Peer asserts that he "could never be called a major sinner," the Button-molder replies:

> But, my friend, that precisely *is* your offense.
> You aren't a sinner in the larger sense;
> That's why you're let off the fiery griddle [i.e., hell]
> And go, like the rest, in the casting ladle....

> You're average then, just middling fair....
> There's more to sin than making a mess;
> A sin calls for vigor and seriousness....
> Now *you* were planned as a shining button
> On the vest of the world, but your loop gave way....
> Yourself is what you've never been—
> So what difference to you to get melted down? (183, 184, 185)

The Button-molder's condemnation is the Norwegian version of Dante's Neutrals in his *Divine Comedy*, whom Dante witnesses just within the Gates of Hell but not residing in Hell Proper. It is a miserable place where Dante's guide, Virgil, claims to house

> the wretched souls of those who lived without disgrace and without praise. They are mixed with that caitiff choir of the angels who were not rebels, not faithful to God, but were for themselves. The heavens drove them forth, not to be less fair, and the depth of Hell does not receive them lest the wicked have some glory over them.... They have no hope of death, and so abject is their blind life that they are envious of every other lot. The world suffers no report of them to live. Pity and justice despise them.

Dante then looks and sees

> a whirling banner which ran so fast that it seemed as if it could never make a stand, and behind it came so long a train of people that I should never have believed death had undone so many.... I...at once and with certainty... perceived that this was the worthless crew that is hateful

> to God and to His enemies. Those wretches, who never were alive.[15]

Dante critic John Sinclair writes that

> these innumerable seekers of safety first, and last, who take no risk either of suffering in a good cause or of scandal in a bad one, are here manifestly, nakedly, that which they were in life, the waste and rubbish of the universe, of no account to the world, unfit for Heaven and barely admitted to Hell. They have no need to die, for they "never were alive." They follow still, as they have always done, a meaningless, shifting banner that never stands for anything because it never stands at all.[16]

Just as Ibsen—who wrote *Peer Gynt* in Rome and Sorrento, Italy—was no doubt familiar with Italy's most renowned poet and epic poem, Dante's *Divine Comedy*, so too both writers were intimately familiar with the Bible. Editorial notes to the *Divine Comedy* link the above passage from Dante's *Inferno* to a passage from the Book of Revelation, when John the Divine is commanded to write to the church of Laodiceans: "I know thy works, that thou art neither cold nor hot: I would thou wert cold or hot. Because thou art lukewarm, and neither cold nor hot, I will spue thee out of my mouth."[17]

The sentiment is certainly advanced by Luther in a letter to a colleague, but with a Protestant edge: "God does not save those who are imaginary sinners. Be a sinner, and let your sins

[15] Dante, *Inferno*, tr. John Sinclair (New York: Oxford University Press, 1961) Canto 3, ll. 35-64.

[16] Dante, pp. 54-55.

[17] Revelation 3:15-16.

be bold, but let your trust in God be bolder."[18] In other words, it's better to be any kind of sinner (whose subsequent penitence may stand *for* something) instead of a lukewarm one. All Peer needed to maintain his status as a lukewarm human being were deception and self-deception or, in Peer's own words, "To know that behind you always lies/A bridge secured for your retreat" (99).

Shocked yet still not fully aware that he has never really made a committed or deliberate choice in his life that may prove the mettle of a human being, Peer seeks to buy time from the Button-molder's judgment to seek affidavits as to his status as either self-conscious sinner or saint. The Button-molder agrees to meet him at "The next crossroads; not a step beyond" (197). Peer then sees the Troll-king, who fails to give Peer such an affidavit because (and these are Peer's words) "I never took the ultimate step./And a man's made of just that kind of thing" (191). In other words, Peer never fully committed even to the half-existence of the troll world—but what's more important here is that he's beginning to know the value of being committed to anything, even to a sin.

At Peer's next crossroads, the Button-molder tells Peer that "To be yourself is to slay yourself" (195)—that is, in Kierkegaard's words, "To die *to* the world,"[19] "To become nothing before God, *and nevertheless infinitely, unconditionally engaged*" in the world. [20] This sense of nothingness is something that Peer almost began to comprehend in the onion

---

[18] A letter From Luther to Melanchthon Letter, no. 99, 1 August 1521, fr. The Wartburg (Segment), tr. Erika Bullmann Flores fr. Luther's *Saemmtliche Schriften* Dr, ed. Johannes Georg Walch (St. Louis: Concordia Publishing House, N.D.), Vol. 15, cols. 2585-2590.

[19] *Journals and Papers* 2:125 (X^3 A 373, n.d., 1850).

[20] Kierkegaard, *For Self-Examination,* 106.

scene before sliding back once again. He admits to his inability to slay his selfish, trollish self so as to become a truer, more transparent self; he despairingly says "I fear I was dead long before I died" (205), echoing Dante's allusion to Revelation, which asserts: "Thou hast a name that thou livest, and art dead."[21] Nevertheless, he evades the problem of himself still.

Nevertheless, Peer, still buying time, claims that there in fact is "a meaning/To all [his] sins" (206) in the person of Solveig. The Button-molder seizes Peer and admonishes him to "Put your house in order!" (206), before calling out to Peer: "To the third crossroads, Peer; but *then*—!" (207).

The ever-merciful Solveig does not condemn Peer as a sinner, but loves him for what he is. And as the sun rises, the Button-molder's voice from behind the hut where Peer and Solveig reside at the end of the play is heard to say, "We'll meet at the final crossroads, Peer; and *then* we'll see—I won't say more" (209). And then Solveig, "her voice rising in the early light" ends the play with the words "Sleep in my arms; I'll watch over thee—/Sleep and dream, my dearest boy!" (209)...and it is as if we audience members or readers are left in the lurch....

Has Peer slayed his selfish self by the end of the play? Or has the ghost of his enabling and loving mother Aase descended in the spirit of Solveig, allowing Peer to continue to sleep and dream his life away?

Ibsen's *Peer Gynt* offers a particularly modern spin on the nature of redemption precisely because we don't know if Peer Gynt is redeemed or not at the end of the play. The ambiguity of Peer's *final* final crossroads, one that happens not on stage but after the play proper has concluded and his life ends, is

---

[21] Revelation 3:1.

essential—otherwise the play would be mere fairy tale. Nevertheless, don't we want Ibsen to tell us what happened to Peer? Don't we want, in effect, to be deceived by an artificial ending, be it happy or sad?

Fortunately, Ibsen is too wise to offer an easy or two-dimensional fairy tale ending. Instead, the playwright invites us to accept the unknown outcome to Peer's life as the unknown outcome to our lives, for, as the Man in Grey reminds us in Act 5, "We're all brothers in old Peer Gynt" (171). In addition, Ibsen—who wrote not for entertainment only—seems also to suggest this: instead of the prospect of concluding Act 5 with the benefit that we really should be entitled to know what will happen next, perhaps not knowing Peer's outcome invites us to go *beyond* noncommittal Peer himself and choose: *Either* live with the thought of nothingness after the stage lights fade / *Or* live with some hope or belief that the mystery of grace will illuminate an exit sign.

4

The Sufferer in Fyodor Dostoevsky's *The Brothers Karamazov*[1]

Introduction

The plot of Fyodor Dostoevsky's last and finest novel revolves around the accusations against and trial of a passionate and decadent son, Dmitri Karamazov, for the murder of his passionate and decadent father, Fyodor. The swirling action delves into the depraved lives and community in which the Karamazov family dwell (both son and twice-widowed father, for instance, are in love with the same woman; issues of greed and inheritance abound). At the center of all the hubbub is the (quite civil) clash between two other Karamazov brothers: the religiously striving Alyosha and the intellectual powerhouse of 19th century secular reason, Ivan.

The story becomes particularly gripping when readers come to realize that, according to Dostoevsky, the world is made up of believers and nonbelievers; and the more cogent the case against Christianity that Dostoevsky makes through the voices of his non-believing characters, the more meaningful the case for Christianity he makes for striving believers. And although Dostoevsky's sympathies fall on the side of the struggling believer, he never soft-peddles the powerful force

[1] Fyodor Dostoevsky, *The Brothers Karamazov*, trs. Richard Pevear and Larissa Volokhonsky (New York: Knopf, 1990). Page numbers will be cited following quoted passages.

and rationale of critics of Christianity that abound in his writings and his time—rendering his works compelling for nonbelievers and believers alike.

One: Life and works of Dostoevsky

Dostoevsky was born in Moscow in 1821, during a time in western and Russian history when popular religious sentiment was rapidly dying and being embalmed by modern secularization.

The Enlightenment that began in the 18th century had come to enthrone the hard sciences, elevating chemistry, the scientific method, and the categorization and compartmentalization of everything measurable. It thus became one of three fundamental death knells in the 19th century for anything considered infinite, like the human spirit or a transcendent divinity. In *The Brothers Karamazov*, Father Zosima makes this clear: "They have science, and in science only that which is subject to the senses. But the spiritual world, the higher half of man's being, is altogether rejected, banished with a sort of triumph, even with hatred" (313).

The second death knell sounds with the Romantic Age, which refuted the Enlightenment's desire to compartmentalize everything. Along pre-Christian and classical Greek and Roman models, many secular romanticists nevertheless also participated in dethroning religion and divinity with paeans to the human imagination and the natural world.

The Industrial Age was the third and final death knell to popular religious sentiment in the 19th century and beyond. This pragmatic age was congruent with the Enlightenment and directed by idealistic, romantic entrepreneurs. Trains and railroads of the Industrial Age thus became the perfect metaphor for Dostoevsky. With it, he began developing the theme that man could live by the finite freedom that materialism offers. A character in one of Dostoevsky's novels portrays trains as "hurrying, clanging, banging, and speeding, they say, for the happiness of mankind!" Then a "secluded thinker" retorts: "It's getting much too noisy and industrial in mankind, there is too little spiritual peace." Another triumphant promoter of progress replies: "Yes, but the banging of carts delivering bread for hungry mankind may be better than spiritual peace."[2] (In another novel, Dostoevsky has a character ponder how "the rumble of carts bringing bread to mankind" is nowadays being construed as "more useful than" Raphael's portrait entitled "Sistine Madonna."[3] This argument fully blossoms in "The Grand Inquisitor" episode of *The Brothers Karamazov*.)

A brief look at Dostoevsky's own life offers abundant clues as to how he so successfully managed to portray the clash between infinite religious freedom and lesser, more finite freedoms offered by secularists and scientific determinists.

•

Amid the hubbub of the busy, bustling, enlightened, romantic, and industrial 19th century, the Dostoevsky family was pious and the author grew up in as much of a religious household as could then be imagined. According to biographer Joseph Frank, Dostoevsky knew the Gospels from early childhood on and heard many stories of the saints; his relation to the peasantry and their religious rituals and storytelling was natural and "nourished Dostoevsky's unshakeable conviction

---

[2] Fyodor Dostoevsky, *The Idiot*, trs. Richard Pevear and Larissa Volokhonsky (New York: Knopf, 2003) 375.

[3] Fyodor Dostoevsky, *Demons*, trs. Richard Pevear and Larissa Volokhonsky (New York: Knopf, 2000) 216.

that the soul of the Russian peasant was imbued with the Christian ethos of love and self-sacrifice."[4]

At age 15 and shortly after his mother died, Dostoevsky entered the St. Petersburg Academy of Military Engineering. Frank notes that, at this critical and highly conflicted time of his life in which he grieved his mother's death and found military engineering a "bleak" prospect, Dostoevsky, "without any apparent cause…lost his voice and seemed to have contracted some throat or chest ailment whose diagnosis was uncertain. [5] Two years later, his father died—assumed murdered by serfs (this last fact is arguably the genesis of the parricide in *The Brothers Karamazov*). Despite all these sorrows, in 1844 and at age 23, Dostoevsky graduated from the military academy but then resigns a military commission to pursue a literary career. When he lost his physical voice amid the suffering of the death of his mother and his reluctance to become part of Russia's military industrial complex, he was on the brink of discovering his true literary voice that would champion love and self-sacrifice in many subsequent novels.

Dostoevsky's first novel, *Poor Folk*, was published a year after graduation. It earned him immediate acclaim by highly influential secular intellectuals of Russia who saw the novel as sympathizing with a brand of socialism that Dostoevsky then believed might include Christ into the mix. Like many young authors, Dostoevsky was simply happy to be recognized, despite that he was comporting with a socialist ideology that

[4] Joseph Frank, *Dostoevsky: A Writer in His Time* (Princeton: Princeton University Press, 2010) 24, 26-27.

[5] Frank, 38.

ultimately rejected religious sentiment, which led to the secularization of Russia's body politic.[6]

Between 1844 and 1849, Dostoevsky engaged in various secular, radical literary groups—all critical of Tsar Nicholas I—until he was arrested as part of a group of thinkers that authorities regarded as a growing insurgency against serfdom and the Tsar. Dostoevsky was sentenced to execution, which was stayed. He instead served four years of hard labor in Siberia, followed by four years in Siberian exile before eventually marrying and returning to St. Petersburg.

He suffered a pivotal life experience during this time, in which he looked in the face of his own mortality and death: Tsar Nicholas I staged a mock execution meant to intimidate the upstart insurgents. A second pivotal event involved Dostoevsky reading the New Testament and seeing what it offered to even the lowliest and most hopeless of prisoners in Siberia. (The only book Dostoevsky had with him for the four years of his penal sentence was a copy of the New Testament.[7]) Frank notes that if Dostoevsky

> had acquired any new convictions at all during the searing experiences of his [arrest, mock execution, and hard labor in Siberia], it was to convince him of two ineluctable truths. One was that the human psyche would never, under any conditions, surrender its desire to assert its freedom; the other was that a Christian morality of love

[6] Such a revolutionary political shift was not limited to Russia. The 1840s saw tectonic shifts from more religiously-based and monarchical systems of government to more secularized and democratized political states throughout Europe, led in great part by France—the Western country Dostoevsky satirizes most in his writings because its culture and language had the greatest secular influence upon 18th and 19th century Russian culture.

[7] See *Demons*, 723n.

> and self-sacrifice was a supreme necessity for both the individual and society. Without these inherited moral values, life among the peasant convicts would have been...hell for Dostoevsky, and he shuddered at the thought that it was precisely *these* values the radicals had now set to undermine and destroy.[8]

Such experiences of secularism and materialism wrought by temporarily aligning himself with secular insurgents and, conversely, experiences of Christian belief while imprisoned came to be the bookends of Dostoevsky's thinking and writings in his post-Siberian years, from his memoir of penal servitude (*Notes from a Dead House*); to his extraordinary conversion novella, *Notes from Underground*, when he breaks entirely free of socialism rooted in secularism; to his most popular novel, *Crime and Punishment*, which hones his critique of the rational and egoistic tactics of secular culture over and against New Testament Christianity; to three big novels that continued to expose the pervading nihilism of 19th century Russian and western culture, namely, *The Idiot*, *Demons*, and *The Adolescent*. Finally, his seminal and ultimate novel, *The Brothers Karamazov*, was completed a year before he died in 1881 at the age of 60 from a lung hemorrhage.

Shortly before these last five big novels were written, his first wife and brother died. Three years later, he married again. He then suffered the death of a first daughter shortly after her birth, had a second daughter and a son, and then suffered the death of a second son, Alexy (nickname: Alyosha), when the boy was three years old. He dedicated *The Brothers Karamazov* to his second wife, Anna, who had helped him stave off a

---

[8] Frank, 283-84.

gambling addiction as well as creditors, set him back on his feet, and had given him a family.

Frank notes that on Dostoevsky's deathbed, he asked that his

> children be summoned, and they kissed him while he gave them his final blessing, enjoining them always to love and obey their mother. He requested that his copy of the New Testament be given to his son Fedya and that the parable of the Prodigal Son be read to the children. [He then told them] that, if they should ever commit a crime (*prestuplenie* has a wider meaning than merely a legal offense) to trust God as their Father, plead with him for forgiveness, and be certain that he would rejoice in their repentance, just as the father had done on the return of the Prodigal Son. It was this parable of transgression, repentance, and forgiveness that he wished to leave as a last heritage to his children, and it may well be seen as his own ultimate understanding of the meaning of his life and the message of his work.[9]

Finally, Frank notes that during mass at Dostoevsky's funeral, the officiating Father "spoke a few words about his friend, all of whose work as a novelist, he said quite acutely, was an echo of Christ's Sermon on the Mount."[10] It could also be added that Dostoevsky's fiction was an extended dramatization of and meditation on the Ten Commandments and the two love commandments, namely, to love God and to love your neighbor as you love yourself.

---

[9] Frank, 925.

[10] Frank, 931.

Two: Ivan Karamazov

A sentence that Dostoevsky wrote about himself in a letter to a dejected friend many years before he conceived the character of Ivan Karamazov is an early template of Ivan: "I am a child of the century, a child of disbelief and doubt, I am that today and (I know it) will remain so until the grave." What kept Dostoevsky from turning into an "Ivan"—and, in addition, what allowed him to maintain a certain artistic objectivity to write something as extraordinarily balanced as *The Brothers Karamazov*—was that his religious faith continued to be strengthened both because of and despite the death knells that tolled over the apparent corpse of religious sentiment in the enlightened, romantic, industrial, secular 19th century. The next sentences in Dostoevsky's letter to his friend confirm such an understanding of his faith:

> "How much terrible torture this thirst for faith has cost me even now, which is all the stronger in my soul the more arguments I can find against it. And yet, God sends me sometimes instants when I am completely calm; at those instants I love and feel loved by others.... Even more, if someone proved to me that Christ is outside the truth, and that *in reality* the truth were outside of Christ, then I should prefer to remain with Christ rather than with the truth."[11]

In sentences like these, Dostoevsky sides with the personality and passion of the young monastic novice, Alyosha Karamazov—but not without sympathizing, as Alyosha does, with his brother, Ivan—the latter being, after all, very much a child of his century, a child of disbelief and doubt, and (Ivan knows it) will remain so until the grave. With the help of the

---

[11] Frank, 220.

Ivan-like intellectual sentiment fermenting in Russia's burgeoning secular culture, Dostoevsky was inspired to make the strongest arguments against Christian belief—all, however, in what he believed to be the service of strengthening the passion of New Testament Christian faith. Perhaps his belief that he was a child of disbelief and doubt was what led him to recognize that faith must always be, as Kierkegaard notes, "a restless thing,"[12] especially when the culture endorses religious doubt, faith in science, and the positioning of commodities above all else. In his late notebooks, Dostoevsky writes: "it is not like a child that I believe in Christ and profess faith in him, but rather, my *hosanna* has come through the great *crucible of doubt*, as the devil says in [*The Brothers Karamazov*]."[13] For Dostoevsky, Frank notes, "intense religious commitment could be combined with a frank confession of the torments of doubt; genuine faith for Dostoevsky would…never be confused with a tranquil acceptance of dogma."[14]

This great crucible of doubt on which Dostoevsky made his religious conversion thereby cast a highly critical eye at primary worldly institutions and dogma administrated under the auspices of the Christian faith, including German and Scandinavian Protestant Lutheranism as well as Roman Catholicism.

Although Alyosha shows some signs of being a closet Lutheran, Dostoevsky—through his own voice and various characters' voices in many of his novels—had little to say about Lutheranism and even less to say about Roman Catholicism. His own eccentric brand of Russian Orthodox Christianity finds its locus not so much in institutional dogma

---

[12] *For Self-Examination*, 17 (XII 308).

[13] Frank, 913.

[14] Frank, 54.

as much as in fundamental precepts of love of God and neighbor-love modeled by Christ in the New Testament. He took seriously (as Melville did in his own seminal book, *Moby-Dick*) the two love commandments on which Christ claims to hang all the laws and the prophets.[15]

Although Dostoevsky understood that Lutheranism, like Russian Orthodoxy, was "a protest against Latin Catholic civilization," Dostoevsky considered Lutheranism as "stupidly contradictory" and containing "nothing positive of its own and ultimately leading to atheism and Nihilism."[16] Ivan Karamazov speaks more specifically to this claim when he tells Alyosha about a man who commits murder, then finds God, and on the day of execution is joyful because he is going to the Lord; Ivan then notes that pastors, judges, and philanthropic ladies of the execution gallery all agree "and his head is whacked off in brotherly fashion, forasmuch as grace has descended upon him, too." Ivan concludes by noting that he read this story in "a little pamphlet…translated into Russian by some Russian Lutheranizing philanthropists from high society and sent out gratis" (240).

Ivan's complaint here perhaps reflects Dostoevsky's own attack against Lutherans—namely, the capability of Lutherans, in a confusion of religion and politics from which Kierkegaard also accused Lutherans of suffering, to advocate for grace and forgiveness of sins on the one hand and capital punishment by gruesome beheading on the other. Perhaps, however, Dostoevsky's assertion of Lutheranism as "stupidly contradictory" need not be expressed in such dramatic brushstrokes. The more garden-variety example of self-professed Lutherans becoming overly dependent upon grace to save the soul at the

---

[15] Matthew 22:39-40.

[16] Frank, 560, 744.

last moment instead of pursuing the hard work of contrition and repentance that true faith exacts would offer a similar critique of poorly practiced Lutheranism.

Elsewhere, Zosima speaks of Lutheran lands (like Rome earlier) being composed of churches that have "disappeared" completely, leaving "just churchmen and splendid church buildings" (65)—something of which Kierkegaard also was critical in 19th century Lutheran Denmark, especially in a time when state churches were not simply religious institutions but informed by the state's body politic. Nevertheless, the narrator of *The Brothers Karamazov* describes Alyosha's sense of faith in Protestant language, namely, that "faith is not born from miracles, but miracles from faith" (26). But whatever the case, the earthly institution of Lutheran Protestantism had, for Dostoevsky, its earthly limitations and contradictions, not unlike Catholicism—the latter of which became the ultimate target of Dostoevsky's attack against institutionalized Christendom, an institution which could dilute, Dostoevsky believed, New Testament Christianity to the point of unrecognizability. As Dostoevsky translators Richard Pevear and Larissa Volokhonsky note: "the announcement at the first Vatican council (1870) of the new dogma of papal infallibility deeply shocked [Dostoevsky]; he saw it as the proclaiming of a 'new Christ' who represents earthly power and has thus succumbed to the third temptation of the devil (see Matthew 4:1-11, Luke 4:1-13)." [17] It was no doubt this papal announcement that compelled Dostoevsky to attack Roman Catholicism so directly in his writings during the final decade of his life, including the novels *Demons*, *The Adolescent*, and *The Brothers Karamazov*. Dependency on material comfort, safety, security, convenience, speed, and ease were funda-

---

[17] *Demons*, 249n.16.

mentally at odds with the spiritual freedom that Christ championed in the wilderness and promoted during his ministry—a clash that culminates for Dostoevsky in *The Brothers Karamazov* amid his most famous attack, "The Grand Inquisitor."

In this attack, Christ becomes the biggest problem of all for the Grand Inquisitor because Christ's life represents the infinite crashing into the finite world and asserting itself by saying that humans have free will. For the Grand Inquisitor, New Testament Christianity is an offense—better ignored or shrugged off or hated or run out of town than addressed—given that it can't logically be addressed by humanity because it cannot be rationally understood. It can only be believed.

Despite Ivan's bitter interpretations of biblical passages combined with his ironic, ambiguous, artistic, and rhetorical sleights of hand, what makes Ivan and his "Legend of the Grand Inquisitor" so compelling is both Ivan's and the Grand Inquisitor's overall compassion for the worldly suffering of innocents and their general love of mankind in this world. That said, Ivan's protest against human pain and suffering and his love of humanity in the abstract is also (given his doubts about God's eternal plan) irreconcilable with the concrete Christian acts of self-love, love of neighbor, and love of God in an imperfect world. Such love of humanity *in the abstract*, in other words, has the capacity to translate into disgust for humans *in the concrete*. Such translation is evident in Ivan, who doesn't much love himself, nor others, nor God, and such irreconcilability ultimately renders him more demonic than saintly, save for his nagging conscience.

The narrator's initial portrait of Dostoevsky's most famous and most excruciatingly conscientious doubter and intellectual is telling. In the middle of the third chapter of the book, Alyosha and Ivan's stepfather, Yefim Petrovich (who cares for the two boys after they were abandoned by Fyodor), is described has having *loved* Alyosha, yet only *seeing genius* in Ivan. In other words, Ivan is brilliant, but hard to love. Even as a child, he was "gloomy and withdrawn, far from timid, but as if he had already perceived by the age of ten that they were indeed living in someone else's family and on someone else's charity, that their father was such that it was a shame to speak of him" (15). Even this detail regarding Ivan's sense of shame towards his father foreshadows his future thoughts and actions against Fyodor. It also resonates with Zosima's notion that shame is "the cause of everything" tragic (43).

In Book 5, readers begin to become acquainted with Ivan, especially how he may accept the existence of God but not the world God created—a world in which so many innocent children suffer (235). In an extraordinary display of Ivan's tortured interior life that he articulates in the last sentence of an episode preceding two critical chapters ("Rebellion" and "The Grand Inquisitor"), Ivan says to Alyosha: "'It's not that I want to corrupt you and push you off your foundation; perhaps I want to be healed by you,' Ivan suddenly smiled just like a meek little boy. Never had Alyosha seen him smile that way" (236). Then, in the next sentence, which is the first and nearly perfect introductory sentiment beginning the episode appropriately called "Rebellion," Ivan tells Alyosha, in direct rebellion against the second love commandment (and, by extension, the first): "I must make an admission…I never could understand how it's possible to love one's neighbors. In my opinion, it is precisely one's neighbors that one cannot possibly love. Perhaps if they weren't so nigh" (236). Here is Ivan in a nutshell: he is capable of loving in the abstract, of being utterly concerned about humanity in the abstract (see, e.g., 237), and of being willing to devote his intellectual powers to the development of grand social schemes and social justice—yet he harbors a certain loathing of and discomfort with those nearby, a loathing and discomfort that extends both to him and to God, the latter of whom he "hastens to return his ticket" into heaven and instead opts to "remain with [his] unrequited suffering and [his] unquenched indignation, *even if [he is] wrong*" (245). Rather than learning to love individually, intimately, and concretely with his heart, he has only developed his rational mind and reason, a condition exceeded only by one other character in the book, namely, Smerdyakov (Ivan's doppelgänger in more ways than one, given that they were born in the same year by a demonic and sensualist father who presumably raped Smerdyakov's mother and ravaged Ivan's mother).

For all of Ivan's passion for and commitment toward a doubt that borders not on healthy skepticism but rather a slippery slope of unleashed cynicism, he does have a conscience. He is no sociopath. Although he asserts that he is not his brother Dmitri's keeper (31), he is not blind to Zosima's notion that each individual is guilty in everything before everyone (289); in Book 11, entitled "Brother Ivan Fyodorovich," he is tormented by his active or passive role in the murder of his father (e.g., 617, 624). The same Ivan who always wishes that his neighbor was not so nigh and even allows a drunken pauper with whom he crosses paths to potentially freeze to death (621)—this same Ivan ultimately re-crosses paths with the unconscious peasant and turns Good Samaritan (633). In other words, perhaps Ivan sees in himself what he doesn't like to see in his conception of God, namely, an authority that turns his back on suffering. Whatever the case, he alters his behavior accordingly and, whether he knows it or not or likes it or not, he behaves ethically. Perhaps he also considers that, had he allowed this drunken peasant to die instead of helping the man, it would be like allowing, either consciously or subconsciously, his drunken father to be murdered.

These moral actions override Ivan's immoral or amoral sense of the universe and ultimately wreak havoc with Ivan's conscience, his arguments against free will, and his nihilistic motto that "everything is permitted."[18]

When Ivan tells Alyosha his dream of the Devil, he describes what the Devil (and presumably Ivan in his darker moments) thinks of conscience. Ivan says, "He [the Devil] taunted me! And cleverly, you know, very cleverly: 'Conscience!' [the Devil says,] 'What is conscience? I make it up myself. Why do I suffer then? Out of universal human habit over seven thousand years. So let us get out of the habit, and we shall be gods!' He said that, he said that!" (653). Two pages later, Alyosha offers a fitting diagnosis of Ivan's illness: "The torment of a proud decision, a deep conscience!" Then the narrator speaks presumably what Alyosha thinks: "God, in whom he [Ivan] did not believe, and his truth were overcoming his heart, which still did not want to submit [to God]." Alyosha then offers an either/or prognosis: Ivan will either "rise into the light of truth" (by confession) or "take revenge upon himself and everyone for having served something he does not believe in" (655). Frank notes that

> numerous commentators have understandably stressed the moving pathos of Ivan's humanitarianism; it has even been suggested...that Dostoevsky was really of the devil's

---

[18] According to critic Diane Thompson, the motto "everything is permitted" is "a verbatim quotation from [I] Corinthians (6:12, 10:23) where Paul uses it polemically to reprove those who have falsely interpreted the true nature of Christian freedom. (Diane Thompson, *The Brothers Karamazov: The Poetics of Memory* (Cambridge: Cambridge University Press, 1991) 154.)

> party and could not suppress his emotional agreement with Ivan. There is no question that Dostoevsky poured into these passages all his own anguish over the abominations he was recording. However, Ivan represents, on the highest level of intellectual and moral sensibility, the supreme and most poignant dramatization of the conflict between reason and faith at the heart of the book, and it would have been inconsistent with his thematic aim to have softened or weakened his utterances. Faith, as Dostoevsky wishes it to be felt in *The Brothers Karamazov*, must be...a commitment supported by nothing except a devotion to the image and example of Christ, and the opposing arguments of reason must thus be given at their fullest strength.[19]

Three: Father Zosima

The counterpoint in *The Brothers Karamazov* to Ivan's nihilism is Father Zosima, one of many religious figures developed in Dostoevsky's novels as examples of self-sacrifice, humiliation, self-knowledge, striving, and gratitude that thrive in dark worlds of self-interest, ego, self-deceit, self-satisfaction, and thanklessness. If Dostoevsky's novels are comparable to mountains of black coal, the pressure at the center of each mountain always yields small but illustrious diamonds, like Sonya in *Crime and Punishment*, Prince Myshkin in *The Idiot*, Tikhon in *Demons*, Makar in *The Adolescent*, and, in *The Brothers Karamazov*, Zosima. Their extraordinarily kind, gentle, innocent, and illuminating characters are diamonds, which, as any seller of diamonds may attest to, are best presented when the velvety backdrop in the casing is darkest.

---

[19] Frank, 871-72.

Halfway through the novel, Zosima, the aged and largely respected religious monk, dies. Over the course of a few days, his corpse emits an odor that his detractors and critics believe to be evidence of an unsaintly soul. By this natural odor and the detractors' naturally odious rumors and superstitions in response to it, however, Alyosha's faith eventually comes to be tested and deepened—a spiritual trial that might be considered the ultimate goal of Zosima's life and teachings. A passage from Thomas Hardy's poem "In Tenebris [In Darkness] (II)" seems particularly fitting: "If a way to the Better there be, it exacts a full look at the Worst."[20]

Passages from the "Odor of Corruption" episode also serve to envision the dark door and threshold of faith through which Dostoevsky wants readers to pass. There exists, however, a salient companion image of this "odor of corruption" that is worthy of mention. It is portrayed in one of Dostoevsky's other novels, *The Idiot*, and it describes a painting of Christ's decaying body after death and also describes Dostoevsky seeing the painting. In *The Idiot*, a young nihilist named Ippolit describes the painting to the novel's near Christlike protagonist, Prince Myshkin:

> "In the picture the face [of Christ] is horribly hurt by blows, swollen, with horrible, swollen, and bloody bruises, the eyelids are open, the eyes crossed; the large, open whites have a sort of deathly, glassy shine. But, strangely, when you look at the corpse of this tortured man, a particular and curious question arises: if all his disciples, his chief future apostles, if the women who followed him and stood by the cross, if all those who believed in him and worshipped him had seen a corpse like that (and it

---

[20] Thomas Hardy, *The Complete Poems*, Ed. James Gibson (New York: Palgrave, 2001) 169.

> was bound to be exactly like that), how could they believe, looking at such a corpse, that this sufferer would resurrect? Here the notion involuntarily occurs to you that if death is so terrible and the laws of nature are so powerful, how can they be overcome?"[21]

This is the door and threshold of faith through which Zosima's life and teachings—set against the natural odor of his corpse—ushers readers. This is, in the end, where the apostle John wants to take readers with words about the corn of wheat dying to bring forth fruit (12:24) that Dostoevsky uses as an epigram to begin his novel. Both want to take readers to this darkest room, to the thought of death and meaninglessness and nothingness itself, for only there might readers glimpse a light through a keyhole in a door under a threshold that stands between mortal life and, in Zosima's words, "a new, infinite, unknown, but swiftly approaching life" (292).

•

One of Zosima's teachings could perhaps be an epigram to the whole of Dostoevsky's writings (for Dostoevsky, like Kierkegaard, was forever interested in how easily we come to deceive others and ourselves in pursuit of avoiding the difficult task of becoming fully human and ethically transparent individuals). Zosima admonishes the Karamazov patriarch, Fyodor: "Above all, do not lie to yourself. A man who lies to himself and listens to his own lie comes to a point where he does not discern any truth either in himself or anywhere around him, and thus falls into disrespect towards himself and others" (44). Given that Zosima knows by personal experience how difficult it is even for earnest self-examination and self-

---

[21] *The Idiot*, 408.

honesty to rout out self-deceptions, and given that he also knows that the world has much less good than ill, Zosima tells Alyosha that the young novice will "behold great sorrow, and in this sorrow [Alyosha] will be happy." Then he says: "Here is a commandment to you: seek happiness in sorrow" (77). These are words emblematic of all of Dostoevsky's works, given that most Dostoevsky characters exemplify despairs from which humans suffer, especially those who attempt to flee from embracing sadness by seeking happiness in the immediate, the sensual, the esthetic, and the worldly without care for the ethical or compassion for anyone.

One of Zosima's most prophetic speeches along this line of thought—prophetic especially in the context of a wireless, digital 21st century—is worth quoting in full. It conjoins technology, science, and secularism to issue a false—or, at best, a time-sensitive and immediate—freedom. Zosima says:

> we are assured that the world is becoming more and more united, is being formed into brotherly communion, by the shortening of distances, by the transmitting of thoughts through the air.[22] Alas, do not believe in such a union of people. Taking freedom to mean the increase and prompt satisfaction of needs, they distort their own nature, for they generate many meaningless and foolish desires, habits, and the most absurd fancies in themselves. They live only for mutual envy, for pleasure seeking and self-display.... And no wonder that instead of freedom they have fallen into slavery, and instead of serving brotherly love and human unity, they have fallen, on the contrary, into *disunity* and isolation.... And therefore the idea of

[22] In 1836, Samuel Morse begins developing the electrical telegraph system, which proves to be the advent of wireless radio communication.

> serving mankind, of the brotherhood and oneness of people, is fading more and more in the world, and indeed the idea now even meets with mockery, for how can one drop one's habits, where will this slave go now that he is so accustomed to satisfying the innumerable needs he himself has invented? He is isolated, and what does he care about the whole? They have succeeded in amassing more and more things, but have less and less joy. (313-14)

That said, Zosima stands firm on not hating "atheists, teachers of evil, materialists, not even those among them who are wicked, nor those who are good, for many of them are good" (164).

How did Zosima come to be so non-judgmental and forgiving? In one passage, he indirectly attributes his development to having learned to read sacred text simply, without outside distractions or commentary from the likes of assistant professors or seminarians or teachers. He calls upon readers of the Scripture reading aloud to children to simply

> begin reading without clever words and without pretension, without putting [your]self above them, but tenderly and meekly, rejoicing that you are reading to them, and that they are listening to you and understand you; loving these words yourself, and only stopping every once in a while to explain some word that a simple person would not understand—do not worry, they will understand everything, the...heart will understand everything. (293)

Reading simply and without distraction—whether it be reading sacred or non-sacred text or the world or the face of a neighbor or the heart of oneself—cannot be overstated. Frank quotes Dostoevsky: "'I came from a pious Russian family.... In our family, we knew the Gospel almost from the cradle.'" The

Dostoevsky children all were taught to read by their mother from a well-known 18th century religious primer, translated from the German and titled *One Hundred and Four Sacred Stories from the Old and New Testaments.* [23] The earliest memories Zosima himself recalls are of his home, family, learning to read from *One Hundred and Four Sacred Stories from the Old and New Testaments*, and of hearing the Bible read aloud, the earliest such reading being a church reading from the book of Job (290-91). Critic Diane Thompson notes,

> Zosima makes the whole world his own ("love every blade of grass") because it all arouses the memory of the Word which he took into his consciousness as a child. Zosima lives in continuous conversation with the Word and he reads the world by it. Everything partakes in a double level of signification, the sacred and the earthly. His whole consciousness is so filled by his memory of the Word, that for him, memory, the Word and consciousness have completely merged and become one and the same.[24]

Zosima thus takes the first sentence of the Gospel of John as his Archimedean point, of the point from which he can leverage and move the whole world. "In the beginning was the Word, and the Word was God."[25] From his own memory of God's word that composes his earliest memories, Zosima gains power to look immediately into the souls of those who come near him and be moved not only to feel compassion for every suffering sorrow that is in another's heart, but to articulate the great and immovable thought that is *compassion for another*. This immovable thought and word, as Zosima's

---

[23] Frank, 23-24.

[24] *Poetics of Memory*, 105.

[25] John 1:1.

close friend Father Paissy tells Alyosha, "lives.... even in the movements of the souls...of atheists" (171). Meanwhile, and according to Zosima's mysterious visitor, it is the vocation of individuals who believe in this great thought and word to not let it die. "We must keep hold of the banner," he says, "and every once in a while, if only individually, a man must suddenly set an example, and draw the soul from its isolation for an act of brotherly communion, though it be within the rank of holy fool" (304). Zosima speaks similarly elsewhere (while also commenting directly upon John's parable of the corn of wheat):

> Only a little seed, a tiny seed is needed: let him cast it into the soul of a simple man, and it will not die, it will live in his soul all his life, hiding there amidst the darkness, amidst the stench of his sins, as a bright point, as a great reminder. And there is no need, no need of much explaining and teaching, he will understand everything simply. (294)

This seed of the great thought of the immovable and holy Word that evokes *compassion* thus becomes central to Zosima's teachings. Such a seed is planted in this finite world but comes from the infinite. Zosima says: "The roots of our thoughts and feelings are not here but in other worlds. That is why philosophers say it is impossible on earth to conceive the essence of things" (320).

Finally, there is an early exchange between Ivan Karamazov and Father Zosima worth considering. The exchange comes after Pyotr Miusov (cousin of Fyodor's first wife, an early benefactor of the Karamazov boys, and an atheist) summarizes to Zosima Ivan's social philosophy that leads to anarchy and the rejection of ethics. Zosima senses that Ivan's thoughts on this issue aren't yet resolved in his heart and thereby torments him. "And there lies your great grief," Zosima says to Ivan, "for it urgently demands resolution." When Ivan smirkingly asks if it can be resolved in himself and, in addition, in a positive way, Zosima says earnestly, "even if it cannot be resolved in a positive way, it will never be resolved in the negative way either—you yourself know this property of your heart, and therein lies the whole of its torment" (70). The "property of the heart" to which Zosima refers and to what Ivan suffers to the point of madness later in the novel is what Frank calls "the image of conscience as a natural and instinctive regulator of the human psyche, whose distortion or perversion leads to a literal 'sickness' of the self, [which was] one of the major themes of the great works of Dostoevsky."[26] Zosima then makes this remarkable assertion to Ivan: "But thank the Creator that he has given you a lofty heart, capable of being tormented by such a torment, 'to set your mind on things that are above, for our true homeland is in heaven' [a conflation of Colossians 3:2 and Philippians 3:20]" (70).

Regarding Zosima's response, Hong writes that "in the face of humankind's common disease, despair, …Pascal notes that 'the greatness of man is great in that he knows himself to be miserable. A tree does not know itself to be miserable. It is then being miserable to know oneself to be miserable; but it is also being great to know that one is miserable.' [Such] despair…is a negative mark of being a creature of possibility, intended to become genuinely human."[27]

Here we arrive at the nexus between the Word and abject despair, a sort of keyhole through which some radical

---

[26] Frank, 226.

[27] Howard Hong, "Trying to do the Right Thing," fr. *Reece Report*, v. 7, no. 1. Northfield, MN, 9, 18 (Pascal passage quoted from his *Pensees*, #397).

light of human possibility amid dark actualities of this world may be spied, a threshold that connects the finite and the infinite. Zosima's first childhood memory of a biblical text is from the book of Job and the great problem that is Job's great sorrow. Zosima's own conclusion to the problem of Job has something to do with connecting the promise of the eternal truth of the Word to the "passing earthly image" of Job's monumental suffering: "What is great here," Zosima says of Job, "is this very mystery—that the passing earthly image and eternal truth here touched each other" (292).

Considered against the backdrop of Zosima's earliest memory of the Word as uttered in the Book of Job, the crossing that is Zosima's life to death, like Job's life and suffering, is a blessed one by virtue of suffering. Zosima says:

> The old grief, by a great mystery of human life, gradually passes into quiet, tender joy; instead of young, ebullient blood comes a mild, serene old age: I bless the sun's rising each day and my heart sings to it as before, but now I love its setting even more, its long slanting rays, and with them quiet, mild, tender memories, dear images from the whole of a long and blessed life.... My life is coming to an end, I know and sense it, but I feel with every day that is left me how my earthly life is already touching a new, infinite, unknown, but swiftly approaching life, anticipating which my soul trembles with rapture, my mind is radiant, and my heart weeps joyfully. (292)

Four: Alyosha Karamazov

Dostoevsky was the kind of observer Kierkegaard had in mind when the Danish author wrote that "if an observer will only pay attention to himself, he will have enough with five men, five women, and ten children for the discovery of all possible states of the human soul."[28] In this context, *The Brother Karamazov*—which addresses what it means to be and become a human being in the crisis-driven 19th century and beyond—is about a particular young man, five or so men and women with whom the young man crosses paths, and ten or so children the young man befriends at the story's end.

The particular young man referred to here is Alyosha, whom the narrator identifies in the first sentence of the book as the hero of the story. Had the narrator not described Alyosha this way, directing the reader to consider the young novice's primary significance to the novel from the outset, *The Brothers Karamazov* could easily have been interpreted as something other than what the book primarily and essentially is. The oldest brother, Dmitri, might have taken this lead role (he does in the Hollywood movie version)—he being the tragic hero of the romance-detective thriller-murder mystery that the book secondarily is. Or perhaps the middle brother, Ivan, could have at least shared top-billing with Dmitri, Ivan being a tragic hero along the lines of a finely wrought Greek tragedy—which the book also is, but again, only secondarily. Given, however, that the narrator elected the compassionate religious novice Alyosha to be his hero, the novel is destined to be from first to last not a page-turning thriller nor a profound Greek tragedy, but rather a pseudo-Gospel narrative.[29] If the book, however, isn't remembered as a Gospel narrative first and foremost, it is perhaps because so

---

[28] Søren Kierkegaard, *The Concept of Anxiety*, ed. and tr. Reidar Thomte in collaboration with Albert B. Anderson (Princeton: Princeton University Press, 1980) 126 (IV 393).

[29] I am indebted to Diane Thompson for describing the three primary narratives in *The Brothers Karamazov* as detective thriller/murder mystery, a piece of classical tragedy, and Gospel narrative. See *Poetics of Memory*, 54-56.

many critics resist the thought of Dostoevsky as a religious writer. These critics pan Alyosha as a poor or pathetic model of what a hero is supposed to be and do—and such critics would be correct if they judge Alyosha against how a traditional dramatic hero is defined.

Alyosha, in other words, doesn't outwardly do much of anything (dramatic action being a staple of western heroism). He doesn't risk his life in any externally dramatic way to save innocents. He doesn't stand calmly before a firing squad while awaiting to be shot for some manufactured criminal charge. He doesn't take a hill amid a spray of enemy fire and against all odds in a military campaign. Alyosha, in other words, is no esthetic or outward hero. But he is an ethical-religious hero along the lines that Kierkegaard distinguishes between these two kinds of heroes. The religious hero, according to Kierkegaard, is great by *suffering* and not by how the esthetic hero is great, namely, by *conquering*.[30] Religious greatness, in other words, is defined by the depth of inwardness and inward suffering that a personality assumes and not by an outward event of which the hero is principle agent. The religious hero is deemed great not by any outward victories he may have accomplished but by how he survives and takes account of the losses. Dostoevsky writes in one of his notebooks, "To conquer the entire world it suffices to conquer oneself." Of this passage, Frank notes that "self-conquest is thus the highest expression of the freedom of the will, the most exalted goal of the most powerful personality."[31]

Given all that, it is still possible to see even "outward" signs of Alyosha's religious heroism, if only because the narrator's "inside" narrative discloses what is not easily nor

---

[30] *Stages*, 454 (VI 423).

[31] Frank, 598.

visibly seen from the outside, at a distance. Alyosha constantly suffers as he witnesses so much tragedy. It is a wonder that he does not succumb to the familial dysfunction he endures. He suffers the buffoonery of his biological father when Fyodor makes a fool of himself before the world in general and Father Zosima in particular. He suffers vile and false recriminations of enemies determined to debase Zosima. He suffers his own restless faith that is shaken but not crushed by the physical odor of so-called "corruption" emanating from his spiritual father's corpse—a physical odor that some deem more damning than his own biological father's psychical odor of corruption. He suffers his hotheaded and impulsive brother, Dmitri, and his cold-hearted and rational brother, Ivan. He suffers his girlfriend, Lise, whose misunderstanding of the therapeutic value of suffering leads to masochism. He suffers his one-time temptress, Grushenka, and his backstabbing opportunist and monastic peer, Rakitin—and he suffers them all without judging them. He loves them all. To paraphrase once more William Faulkner's compact definition of love, he loves them not *because*, but *despite*—not *because* they are what they are but *despite* that they are what they are.[32] He witnesses and stands in the fire and suffers with all. He feels and suffers the guilt of every guilty party. He is empathetic without being destroyed by his sensitivity. He suffers his world's sins—and he helps save lives *because* he stands in the fire and suffers and feels guilty with all.

When he kisses Ivan after Ivan tells the Legend of the Grand Inquisitor, he establishes a certain freedom from the corruption of the world without actually leaving the world. He maintains a radical goodness even as he dwells amid the actuality of evil. He lives and moves in this world without

---

[32] See p. 42.

being a slave to the world, without being of this world. As Dostoevsky critic Rowan Williams suggests, just as Alyosha's kiss establishes his freedom from Ivan, Christ's kiss of the Grand Inquisitor (from whence Alyosha's kiss is modeled)

> establishes *Christ's* freedom; it literally secures freedom from the prison and it represents the freedom to refuse the argument over power and tragic necessity.... Gratuitous acceptance in the face of rejection has become possible because of Christ; he has not, after all, asked the impossible but has changed the scope of what is possible, and Alyosha acts so as to demonstrate this.[33]

What Williams suggests here is that the freedom Christ and his disciples like Zosima and Alyosha offer is not some impossible life on earth but rather a life that continually evokes the freedom of the *possible* in the human. It is not an unbridled and unrestrained sense of freedom embraced by the likes of Ivan and others who entertain nihilism, one of whom maintains in Dostoevsky's novel *Demons* that "there will be entire freedom when it makes no difference whether one lives or does not live. That is the goal to everything."[34]—This nihilistic sense of freedom turns the universe into a meaningless joke and jest, with God the ultimate jokester and with a bemused humanity the butt of the joke. Such a deathlike freedom is contrary to the spiritual freedom that so offends Ivan and the Grand Inquisitor—a freedom that does not look upon the universe as a meaningless jest but rather as a meaningful gesture, a freedom that allows each person to strive voluntarily in what Zosima calls "this terrible school of

---

[33] Rowen Williams, *Dostoevsky: Language, Faith, and Fiction* (Waco, TX: Baylor University Press, 2008) 31, 32.

[34] *Demons*, 115.

life...in the hope that after the long trial he will achieve self-conquest, self-mastery to such a degree that he will, finally, through a whole life's obedience, attain to perfect freedom—that is, freedom from himself—and avoid the lot of those who live their whole lives without finding themselves in themselves" (28). Victor Frankl would assign such achievement to the tragic optimist, or one who owns "an optimism in the face of tragedy and in view of the human potential which at its best always allows for: (1) turning suffering into a human achievement and accomplishment; (2) deriving from guilt the opportunity to change oneself for the better; and (3) deriving from life's transitoriness an incentive to take responsible action."[35]

By the time of his initial epiphany in the brief but extraordinary "Cana of Galilee" episode, Alyosha is spiritually prepared to take on the world, for he has turned tragic optimist. Like his mentor, Zosima, he is endowed with the Word and the sensitivity and compassion to wield the Word with a remarkable admixture of honesty and ethical measure. And despite the various sufferings Alyosha endures throughout the novel, his essential good nature remains unchanged from the initial description of him in the book. His nature, in other words, never radically alters as he grows; it only deepens. He simply becomes *more himself* by virtue of the sufferings and experiences of adulthood. The teachings he receives from Father Zosima are not so much new illuminations as they are affirmations of things already in him and remembered by him.

The narrator initially describes Alyosha as loving people and living

---

[35] Viktor Frankl, *Man's Search for Meaning* (Boston: Beacon Press, 1992) 139-40.

> all his life, it seemed, with complete faith in people, and yet no one ever considered him either naive or a simpleton.... He accepted everything without the least condemnation, though often with great sadness.... No one could either surprise or frighten him.... Indeed, everyone loved this young man.... He possessed in himself, in his very nature, so to speak, artlessly and directly, the gift of awakening a special love for himself.... He was serene and even-tempered. He never wanted to show off.... He never remembered an offense.... He was always among the best of his class in his studies, but was never the first. (19, 20)

When Alyosha wonders why Zosima sends him out into a profane and corrupt world, he does not fear figuring out how to live *in* such a world without being *of* it. He demands "the truth, seeking it and believing in it, and in that belief demanding immediate participation in it" (26). While his brother Ivan, for instance, bemoans the suffering of children in the abstract but does not seem to have the concrete capacity to do anything about such suffering, Alyosha walks out onto the streets of his village, sees children suffering (even children who may initially believe Alyosha to be an enemy) and instantly begins to attend to their suffering. Zosima tells Alyosha: "You will go forth from these walls, but you will sojourn in the world like a monk. You will have many opponents, but your very enemies will love you. Life will bring you many misfortunes, but through them you will be happy, and you will bless life and cause others to bless it—which is the most important thing" (285).

Before Alyosha begins his own unorthodox ministry in the world, however, he walks in the wilderness of his own trials and temptations as he figures out how to live with and respond to the death of his beloved teacher, Father Zosima.

After Alyosha's dream of the wedding of Cana (in which Zosima bids Alyosha to begin his work), Alyosha awakens and walks out of the cell where his dead teacher lay. His subsequent epiphany shows heaven and earth, the infinite and the finite, freedom and necessity, all merge into a seamless and meaningful whole, which both mimics and confirms Zosima's own conclusion to the great problem of Job that Zosima has carried all his life, namely, "this very mystery—that the passing earthly image and eternal truth here touched each other" (292). Here is how the narrator describes the quiet, earth-shaking scene:

> [Alyosha] did not stop on the porch [of the cell where Zosima lay in state], but went quickly down the steps. Filled with rapture, his soul yearned for freedom, space, vastness.... Alyosha stood gazing and suddenly, as if he had been cut down, threw himself to the earth. He did not know why he was embracing it, he did not try to understand why he longed irresistibly to kiss it, to kiss all of it, but he was kissing it, weeping, sobbing, and watering it with his tears, and he vowed ecstatically to love it, to love it unto ages of ages.... He wanted to forgive everyone and for everything, and to ask forgiveness, oh, not for himself!, but for all and for everything, "as others are asking for me," rang again in his soul. But with each moment he felt clearly and almost tangibly something as firm and immoveable as this heavenly vault descend into his soul. Some sort of idea, as it were, was coming to reign in his mind—now for the whole of his life and unto ages of ages. He fell to the earth a weak youth and rose up a fighter, steadfast for the rest of his life, and he knew it and felt it suddenly. (362-63)

Kissing and embracing the earth just as he kissed and embraced the arch-ideological opponent of his beloved Zosima (his own brother, Ivan), Alyosha sojourns into the world without being of it—that is, without being a sensualist like his father and Dmitri and without being an abstract intellectual and hermit who flees from the world like Ivan. He has, as it were, suffered death in "The Odor of Corruption" episode, yet now walks the earth and ministers to the world's sorrows whenever and wherever it comes "nigh" to him.

Alyosha thus steps out onto the streets of his hometown in the final three books of the novel and begins his ministry in earnest by gathering a group of children, whom the narrator numbers as "about twelve" (768) around him to help them learn to love themselves and their neighbor. He helps them to learn to live *for* others (535-37). He helps them to see how it is possible to bring together apparently irreconcilable parties in Socratic method (indirectly, "as if quite unintentionally and inadvertently") so that, "miracle of miracles," enemies might come to love one another (538). He instructs one of the boys in particular (Kolya) to get to know other people, for getting to know other people "will remake [him] more than anything" (556). The novel ultimately concludes with Alyosha's twelve or so young charges around him, with Alyosha's speech at the stone addressing essentially the need to remember and embrace the first and second love commandments. Just as love presupposes love, goodness ennobles goodness and that, if all else fails, one's projection of a single childhood memory of goodness and innocence may be the only seed necessary—even in a parched and desolate landscape of experience—not only to become human but to inhabit a meaningful life that bears fruit.

Coda

How Professor Howard V. Hong Taught

—A Remembrance—

Note: Dr. Howard V. Hong's 40-plus-year tenure at St. Olaf College began in 1938. During those years, he taught more than 5,000 students in mostly philosophy courses, but also (especially in the 1940s) English and psychology courses. Many of those students took multiple courses under his tutelage. The memoir below includes reflections derived from some of the final courses Dr. Hong taught at St. Olaf, including a January interim course entitled Philosophical Ideas in Literature *(1979) and the final* Kierkegaard *course he taught (February-May 1979). Parts of this remembrance are extracted from the "Foreword" and an essay entitled "One More Visit to the Hong House" from* Toward the Final Crossroads: A Festschrift for Edna and Howard Hong *(Mercer University Press, 2009) and also from a eulogy delivered at the memorial service for Howard Hong at St. Olaf College's Boe Memorial Chapel on March 27, 2010.*

Genius is a late Middle English word, its Latin derivative meaning "an attendant spirit present from one's birth; an innate ability or inclination."

More informally, when I think of what genius is or, more specifically, what the *mark* of genius in a person is, I think of how virtually everything that person says or does in his or her professional persona bears some fundamental, primitive, elemental stamp of that person. Read two or three lines of Shakespeare or Emily Dickinson—and you know it is Shakespeare or Emily Dickinson. Hear a bar or two of Mozart or Wagner or Beethoven—and you know it is Mozart or Wagner or Beethoven. Stand before an Annie Leibovitz or a Picasso and you do not have to look into the corner of the photograph or painting for a signature to know it is a Leibovitz or a Picasso. It is as though men and women of genius reveal their genius through nearly every gesture in the professional field in which their genius blossoms. The genius of a person, then, owns a singular voice, one that can be mimicked or parodied by others but is fully expressed only by the original.

I locate Dr. Hong's professorial genius in his innate ability to engage and deeply respect his students in real time, time and time and time again—which is not to say that you cannot see Dr. Hong and his highly meticulous scholarship in any of the essays or books he wrote, or the translations of and introductions and footnotes to all the Kierkegaard texts on which he and his wife, Edna, worked. It is just that, as a *teacher* of students, his genius was located more in *how* he spoke the words he spoke (which was with a gravity intended always to be weighed by others) and *how* his very presence emulated the words he spoke. He could fill up a room with a presence and a passionate engagement on whatever topic or idea (across a broad-based liberal arts spectrum) that was currently up for review. With his presence came a highly concentrated intensity and singleness of purpose in his message and its delivery in real time.

As for his message, virtually all thoughts, notions, and ideas in any given conversation would eventually be boiled down to one core question: *What does it mean to be, to become a human being?*—and Dr. Hong was economical enough to massage that message to fit any address or lecture or conversation on any occasion at any time to any person with whom he crossed paths. Whenever there was at least one student in his sight, it was as though Dr. Hong, like Diogenes, had a lamp in his hand and was always looking in everyone's eyes for the possibilities within them to become an authentic human being. Or rather, he looked in everyone's eyes for a human being who perhaps needed to hear either for the first time or the umpteenth time the question, "What does it mean to be, to become a human being?"

Then there is within his genius his singular brand of humor and affinity for the absurd; and his constant question-asking relative to the core question of what is means to become a human being; and his ability to so quickly assess any problem from multiple points of view; and his sweeping grasp of history and philosophical anthropology; and even the gleam in his eye whenever he said hello or goodbye to you—all of these things are marks and stamps and tailings of the genius that is Dr. Hong as teacher.

Put it all together in a classroom, and this is what you get:

Dr. Hong would shuffle into class on the fifth floor of St. Olaf College's Holland Hall from the room's only entrance in the back of the room before stopping for a brief moment. His first task was to see what the most recent political science or philosophy or history professor had written on the front blackboard. It only took Dr. Hong a moment to distill whatever good, bad, or ugly ideas were scratched on the slate before he proceeded to the lectern.

He usually had books with him, but they seldom were of any use during his present lecture, for he seldom (if ever) referred to them. I always imagined that his thumb and forefinger had become trapped in the book he was translating one floor above at the time the bell rang for class. He would then scurry downstairs—still caught in his own trap—before temporarily releasing himself from his translations to teach.

In effect, he had no notes. After many years of teaching, he did not need any. Whatever teaching materials he needed on any given day could be scrounged from whatever was already on the chalkboard when he came into the classroom. This method kept his teaching nimble and students could regularly look forward to see an inspired, genuine, passionately engaged teacher give birth to very old and durable ideas and questions that lay beneath the very new and fresh blackboard scrawls.

And although Dr. Hong's lectures were never for entertainment only, a Hong lecture always promised brilliant theater. The subject matter focused on tragic falls, comedic foibles, and joyful possibilities of being and of becoming human, with its most memorable deliveries always employing farce. And like great actors of farce described in Kierkegaard's *Repetition*, Dr. Hong was

> not only able to walk, but he is also able to *come walking*...and by means of this genius he also improvises the whole scenic setting.... [He] is sheer economy..., an incognito in whom dwells the lunatic demon of comedy..., [having] the courage to venture what the individual makes bold to do only when alone, what the mentally deranged do in the presence of everybody, [and] what the genius knows how to do with the authority of genius, certain of laughter.[1]

---

[1] *Repetition*, 161, 163, 164 (III 200, 202, 203).

I know of only one time in which I suspected that this master of farce actually *planted in advance* words and diagrams on the blackboard that he later, in lecture, passed off as some other professor's truisms (if my suspicion was correct, the "offense" certainly would have fallen under the Kierkegaardian ethical categories of *pious fraud*[2] or *deceiving into the truth*[3]—for Dr. Hong's Socratic methods always served the art of helping others ethically give birth to themselves). The occasion was a memorial lecture on the Ides of March in 1988 in the large amphitheater lecture room, Holland Hall 501, and the overall theme of the discussion had to do with the decadence or fallout of western culture since the Renaissance and how such decadence informs the question of what it means to be, to become a human being.

Given that the lecture was the only one of Dr. Hong's that this returning alumnus ever taped, I can let him speak for himself:

> I had some notes here or something—but I don't really need them, because I came in here and I found that some person—bless his or her or their hearts—did it all for me. [Dr. Hong directs the audience's attention to the blackboard, which is filled with mathematical equations, isolated words, and more than a dozen X-Y graphs, *all of which display downward sloping curves from left to right.*] I put a sign here, reading 'Please Don't Erase the Material.' And I wrote 'SAVE' up there [on the board several times]. Now. There you have the whole thing. There are no handouts. You have it all there. [Long pause.] Any questions? [Hall fills with laughter.]

---

[2] *Journals and Papers* 6:6205 (IX A 171).

[3] *The Point of View*, 54 (XIII 541).

Despite the respect an undergraduate ought to give to a professor, I always found myself laughing nervously at whatever the eccentric Dr. Hong said, although I seldom had a clue of what he was talking about at the time (my fault, not his). Nevertheless, it was during those terrific comedic pauses around which he developed his lectures that I realized that Dr. Hong's methods of teaching combined what Thomas Mann calls "anticipatory learning" with a Charlie Chaplin-song-and-dance. And so, by dint of Dr. Hong's innate respect for his students, my job was simply to trust him. If I didn't get the joke at the time, at least I was entertained—and if I thus paid enough attention to the jokes because of the entertainment, I hoped that, by sheer desire to understand the jokes, I would come to know that eventually "getting the joke" meant walking into new thresholds of understanding, knowledge, and wisdom.[4] What others called Dr. Hong's indirect or

[4] Writes Dr. Hong: "Man is uniquely characterized and profoundly defined as the being who laughs. Man, the laughing creature, has called certain baboons laughing baboons simply because their cries approximate the sound of human laughter. The baboon, however, lacks the presupposition of laughter: the discernment of significant differences. Laughter arises essentially from an awareness of contradiction, opposites, basic contrasts. Laughter means discrimination, the distinction between appearance and reality, what is expected and what is, what is and what ought to be" ("The Comic, Satire, Irony, and Humor: Kierkegaardian Reflections" 99). Had I not learned anything more from Dr. Hong about the ethics of what it means to be and to become a human being than the short draught that he distilled above, I would count myself a blessed student. If only we pay attention to those things that make us laugh, and persistently and deeply ask *why* they make us laugh, we may come to see more deeply into the reflecting pool at the bottom of the well of our esthetic, ethical, and religious selves than we now currently know or imagine. We would come to know what Mark Twain meant when he wrote that "Everything human is pathetic. The secret source of

Socratic method, I now took as his penchant for non sequiturs, or the indulgence of apparently meaningless but tantalizing assertions that evoke powerful truths to the attentive audience. Call it what you will, most students took the bait, even if they did not know at the time what they were swallowing.

For Dr. Hong—at least to his students—seldom spoke directly about *anything*. (I'm not a big fan of Polonius in *Hamlet*, but what the character says about indirect communication is as Hongian-Kierkegaardian as it gets: "See you now,/Your bait of falsehood takes this carp of truth,/And thus do we of wisdom and of reach,.../By indirections find directions out."[5]) Whenever he could speak indirectly about a given passage, he did—and his language thereby became highly efficient, highly elastic, highly evocative, and highly lyrical. He was a master of digression, however, he never digressed *from* the topic; he always digressed *to* the topic...via either an anecdote from another Kierkegaard text or a parable of his own making or story about what he saw out the window that morning or (more times than not) a joke. This also humanized and thereby made real and relevant the topic at hand. He also knew what Emerson knew, namely, that a human being "is an analogist, and studies relations in all objects"—and thus "the world is emblematic."[6] To Dr. Hong as teacher, then, the world becomes a great gift and treasure-trove-repository of vehicles to illuminate whatever ideas are presently at hand—and by such indirection, the learner

Humor itself is not joy but sorrow. There is no humor in heaven" (*Pudd'nhead Wilson's New Calendar, Following the Equator* (1897), epigraph to chap. 10.).

[5] *Hamlet*, 2.1.

[6] Emerson, Ralph Waldo, *Essays and Lectures* (New York: Library of America, 1983) 21, 24.

Socratically is allowed and freed up by the teacher to come to the revelatory moment on her or his own terms.

But then, perhaps I am not being quite fair to Dr. Hong, for there were times when he spoke quite directly to his students. Here, for instance, is him speaking to thousands of unassuming freshmen during lectures over scores of years.

~Where am I?—a question of place.
~Where did I come from?—a question of origin.
~Where am I going?—a question of destiny.
~Who am I?—a question of identity.
~Why am I?—a question of purpose.

Granted, these are very direct questions usually brought up in Philosophy 101 courses in college and then quickly forgotten within a week because their maddening simplicity renders them apparently impossible in our sophisticated, highly technological and busy worlds.

But they are not impossible questions. Rather, they are questions that *evoke* the possible, and it is personal struggles for personal answers to those questions that encompass ethical claims upon humans.

For to have a self and to be a self first requires one to know what a self is, and to know what a self is must begin with such questions—this despite our tendencies to defer such questions to some distant tomorrow, primarily because the busyness of our daily lives seeks to choke the life out of such inquiry.

That is why so many claimed Dr. Hong to be St. Olaf's resident Socrates—not that he was the only philosophy professor to ask these questions, because many other professors also asked and continue to ask them. Rather, Dr. Hong is perhaps remembered as the resident Socrates of St. Olaf

College for one simple reason: like the gadfly Socrates claimed to be, Dr. Hong never ceased to ask these questions day after day after day. Not only that, his own brand of this deadly repetitious Socratic method helped forty years of students give birth to themselves. (My personal experience, however, was less obstetrical and more like a mugging. Dr. Hong turned me on my head, shook out trivial trinkets of my half-baked self that I either had quite naturally or quietly and desperately pocketed over the course of my young life, and set me back on my feet. I was left with not much more than empty pockets and the astonishment that I somehow had become richer in the fleecing and a bit more levelheaded for the tumult. I account Dr. Hong's teaching and the method by which he taught the primary fruits of my college career. It modeled all that a true liberal arts education ought to be and do, namely, to help students not to get a job but to get a life—and not just a life but a genuine human existence—that is, to arrive at a place in their own minds and hearts where they may properly begin to become fully human).

First and last, Dr. Hong took his cue from three prototypes. When coming down to the Piraeus—that Athenian marketplace where the mass of humanity trafficked—Socrates tore a hole in the hole of the sophistry that suggested a human being needed things external to oneself—and not simply oneself—in order to know oneself. Dr. Hong also took his cue from Jesus, who, when entering into time and history tore a hole in the hole of the world, thereby exposing the eternal kingdom to the temporal nomadic tribe of humankind. Finally, he took his cue from Kierkegaard who, when walking and talking in the streets of a modern market town tore a hole in the hole of a rapidly accelerating technological, consumer-driven, smug, comfortable, optimistic, unreflective, increasingly inactive and thereby increasingly nonhuman world.

As teacher, Dr. Hong's own *vocatio* thus called upon him to tear holes in the holes of any and every individual student's poorly woven pockets and then steal away with those students' counterfeit selves. Dr. Howard Hong, Master Thief of False Selves, knew that a true self, if clothed at all, must have attire more elemental than the superficial styles of so many false selves. The textile or *textus* of the cloth needs to befit the thought, word, and deed that is one's ethical self; thoughts must be shuttled through the loom of the ethical to produce good words; good words must be dyed and woven into ethically durable colors and tangible patterns of actual deeds.

Postscript

The movement of the religious, according to Søren Kierkegaard, is not "the movement from the simple to the interesting, but from the interesting to the simple."[7]

The essential simplicity of Howard Hong's teaching was that he never stopped with the interesting alone, for he knew that the interesting merely grabs your attention, and anything can do that. The interesting, in other words, is incidental and comes at you from the outside and from every imaginable direction every day in this confusing and contradictory and colorful world.

But Howard didn't just want to be grabbed, only to be grabbed again by the next "interesting" thing that crossed his path. He wanted his attention *held*, for he knew that the only crucial and viable thing that could hold the attention of any person until the end of time was not the incidentally interesting that wades in the shallows of our lives, but the essentially simple that descends into the depths of our very beings.

---

[7] *The Point of View*, 94 (XIII 579).

And so he began to *move*, precisely because he had *become moved* by the simple—which is to say that he not only deliberately chose to become a Christian, he actually began to make the movement of the religious by deliberately choosing it again and again each and every day. He never stopped. It was, on occasion, maddening for some of us even to witness his movements. His tenacious repetition, however, was precisely the kind of movement that was necessary to find meaning in life—for even imagining a meaningless life was a living death to Howard. Repetition, then (and as Kierkegaard suggests), is the very signpost of eternity and thereby the way one moves from the interesting to the simple.

That said, Howard Hong is one the most interesting persons I have ever met. For what else do you call a man who chooses to live a simple life, while also deliberately marrying and committing to the marriage for nearly 70 years, during which time he also committed to learn Danish, raise eight children, manage a home and two north woods cabins, develop and curate a world-class research library, teach thousands of students over the course of more than forty years, and translate and painstakingly edit, footnote, read, or otherwise participate in developing 15,887 pages of text of a difficult Dane? And that is just the primary tier of his accomplishments. The secondary tier includes things like reforesting large tracts of the north woods, reading voraciously, sniffing out the best cheeses in the Midwest, collecting balls of twine....

It's not that he wasn't intimately acquainted with the interesting. In fact, I can't remember a single time when he wasn't responding to the interesting that was always and everywhere swirling around him: worms crawling out of their underground tombs and onto St. Olaf College campus sidewalks each spring ("Look!" he would say like Zorba the

Greek, "It's a miracle!"); a choice passage near the end of Stephen Vincent Benét's "The Devil and Daniel Webster" ("Look!"); the dance of light on Lake Superior waters in front of one of the Hong family summer cabins at 5:30 on a July morning ("Look!"); or—and this stands alone because of his ever-eye-popping expression whenever he saw her—that forever interesting, forever simple Edna ("Look!").

So what is the simple? It is passionate engagement. It is stoic. It is focused. It is saintly. It is plain. It is pure of heart. It is ethical and committed and purposeful and packed full of meaning. It is what Melville calls "mute calm" and "eternal mildness of joy" that exists even "amid the tornadoed Atlantic of [our] being."[8]

How do I know all this? Less from thinking abstractly and more from witnessing concretely the plain and simple example that was Howard's life. Hearing Howard speak and observing him make the simple movements of what Kierkegaard called the "boring categories of the good"[9] was never boring. Why? Because he always sought meaning and he helped students see that *meaning* is never boring. "What does it *mean*"—and then, arms folded, he would look up and squeeze the questions out of himself—"What does it *mean*...to be, to become a human being?" And: "What does *this* word and *this* word and *that* word really *mean*?... What are their *radical* meanings? ...their *root* meanings?" He grabbed you with these apparently impossible questions in such a way that suggested that such questions were by no means impossible but instead simply questions that evoked the possible in us all. And not only that; Howard then held you and continued to hold you until you came to hold yourself.

[8] *Moby-Dick*, Chap. 87.

[9] *The Point of View*, 92 (XIII 577).

Howard Hong

Works Cited

Alighieri, Dante. *Inferno*. Translated by John Sinclair. New York: Oxford University Press, 1961.

Bible, The. King James Version.

Borges, Jorge Luis. *Ficciones*. New York: Grove Press, 1962.

Butler, Samuel. *Samuel Butler's Notebooks*. New York: Dutton, 1951.

Dickinson, Emily. *Final Harvest: Emily Dickinson's Poems*. Edited by Thomas H. Johnson. Boston: Little, Brown, and Co., 1961.

Dostoevsky, Fyodor. *The Brothers Karamazov*. Translated by Richard Pevear and Larissa Volokhonsky. New York: Knopf, 1990.

———. *Demons*. Translated by Richard Pevear and Larissa Volokhonsky. New York: Knopf, 2000.

———. *The Idiot*, Translated by Richard Pevear and Larissa Volokhonsky. New York: Knopf, 2003.

———. *Notes From Underground*. Translated by Richard Pevear and Larissa Volokhonsky. New York: Knopf, 1993.

Dylan, Bob. *Lyrics 1962-2001*. New York: Simon and Schuster, 2004.

Emerson, Ralph Waldo. *Essays and Lectures*. New York: Library of America, 1983.

Frank, Joseph. *Dostoevsky: A Writer in His Time*. Princeton: Princeton University Press, 2010.

Frankl, Victor. *Man's Search for Meaning*. Boston: Beacon Press, 1992.

Gribben, Alan. *Mark Twain's Library*. Boston: Hall, 1980.

Hardy, Thomas. *The Complete Poems*. Edited by James Gibson. New York: Palgrave, 2001.

Harries, Karsten. "Metaphor and Transcendence." In *On Metaphor*, edited by Sheldon Sacks. Chicago: University of Chicago Press, 1979.

Hays, John. *Mark Twain and Religion*. New York: Lang, 1989.

Holiday Magazine. Philadelphia: Curtis Publishing Co., April 1954.

Hong, Howard V. "The Comic, Satire, Irony, and Humor: Kierkegaardian Reflections." In *Midwest Studies in Philosophy* 1. U.S.A.: Blackwell Publishing, 1976.

————. "Trying to do the Right Thing." In *Reece Report*, 7/1. Northfield, Minnesota: Richard Reece, January 1992.

Ibsen, Henrik. *Peer Gynt.* Translated by Rolf Fjelde. Minneapolis: University of Minnesota Press, 1980.

Kierkegaard, Søren. *Kierkegaard's Journals and Notebooks*, vol. 2. George Pattison, volume editor. Princeton: Princeton University Press, 2008.

————. Kierkegaard's Writings series. Howard V. Hong, general editor. Princeton; Princeton University Press, 1978-1998:

III. *Either/Or* I, edited and translated with introduction and notes by Howard V. and Edna H. Hong, 1987.

IV. *Either/Or* II, edited and translated with introduction and notes by Howard V. and Edna H. Hong, 1987.

VI. *Fear and Trembling* and *Repetition*, edited and translated with introduction and notes by Howard V. and Edna H. Hong, 1983.

VIII. *The Concept of Anxiety*, edited and translated with introduction and notes by Reidar Thomte in collaboration with Albert B. Anderson, 1980.

XI. *Stages of Life's Way*, edited and translated with introduction and notes by Howard V. and Edna H. Hong, 1988.

XII. *Concluding Unscientific Postscript to* Philosophical Fragments, edited and translated with introduction and notes by Howard V. and Edna H. Hong, 1992.

XIV. *Two Ages*, edited and translated with introduction and notes by Howard V. and Edna H. Hong, 1978.

XIX. *The Sickness Unto Death*, edited and translated with introduction and notes by Howard V. and Edna H. Hong, 1980.

XXI. *For Self-Examination* and *Judge for Yourself*, edited and translated with introduction and notes by Howard V. and Edna H. Hong, 1990.

XXII. *The Point of View: On My Work as an Author*, edited and translated with introduction and notes by Howard V. and Edna H. Hong, 1998.

XXIII. *The Moment and Late Writings*, edited and translated with introduction and notes by Howard V. and Edna H. Hong, 1998.

XXIV. *The Book on Adler*, edited and translated with introduction and notes by Howard V. and Edna H. Hong, 1998.

————. *Søren Kierkegaard's Journals and Papers*, I-VII. Edited and translated with notes by Howard V. and Edna H. Hong. Commentary by Gregor Malantschuk. Bloomington: Indiana University Press, 1967-1978.

Lorentzen, Jamie. *Sober Cannibals, Drunken Christians: Tragic Optimism in Polarized Worlds*. Macon, GA: Mercer University Press, 2010.

Lorentzen, Jamie. Editor. *Toward the Final Crossroads: A Festschrift for Edna and Howard Hong*. Macon, GA: Mercer University Press, 2009.

Luther, Martin. *Saemmtliche Schriften*, vol. 15. Edited by Johannes Georg Walch. St. Louis: Concordia Publishing House, N.D.

Melville, Herman. *Selected Poems of Herman Melville*. Edited by Robert Penn Warren. Boston: David R. Godine, 2004.

————. The Writings of Herman Melville: The Northwestern-Newberry Edition I. Chicago: Northwestern University Press, 1968-1993.

III. *Mardi and the Voyage Hither*, edited by Harrison Hayford, Hershel Parker, and G. Thomas Tanselle, 1970.

VI. *Moby-Dick, or The Whale*, edited by Harrison Hayford, Hershel Parker, and G. Thomas Tanselle, 1988.

XIV. *Correspondence*, edited by Lynn Horth, 1993.

Milton, John. *Complete Poetry and Major Prose*. Edited by Merritt Y. Hughes. Indianapolis: Odyssey Press, 1957.

Parke, John. "Seven Moby Dicks," *New England Quarterly*. Vol. 28, September 1955.

Parker, Hershel. *Herman Melville: A Biography*, 2 vols. Baltimore: The Johns Hopkins University Press, 1996.

Phipps, William. *Mark Twain's Religion.* Macon, GA: Mercer University Press, 2003.

Shakespeare, William. *The Riverside Shakespeare*. Boston: Houghton Mifflin Company, 1974.

Sontag, Susan. *At the Same Time: Essays and Speeches.* New York: Farrar, Strauss, and Giroux, 2007.

Styron, William. "Huck, Continued" in *The New Yorker*, 25 June 1995.

Thompson, Diane. *The Brothers Karamazov: The Poetics of Memory.* Cambridge: Cambridge University Press, 1991.

Thoreau, Henry David, *Walden and other Writings*. Edited by Joseph Wood Krutch. New York: Bantam Books, 1981.

Trilling, Lionel. *The Liberal Imagination*. New York: Viking, 1950.

Twain, Mark. *The Annotated Huckleberry Finn*. Edited by Michael Patrick Hearn. New York: W. W. Norton, 2001.

————. *The Adventures of Tom Sawyer*. U.S.A.: Library of America, 1982.

————. *The Autobiography of Mark Twain*, 2 vols. Edited by Charles Neider. New York: Harper, 1990.

————. *Following the Equator: A Journey Around the World.* Hartford: American Publishing Company, 1898.

————. *Life on the Mississippi*. U.S.A.: Library of America, 1982.

————. *Tales, Speeches, Essays, and Sketches*. New York: Penguin, 1994.

Vincent, Howard. *The Trying-Out of* Moby-Dick. Carbondale, Illinois: Southern Illinois University Press, 1949.

Williams, Rowen. *Dostoevsky: Language, Faith, and Fiction*. Waco, TX: Baylor University Press, 2008.

Wright, Richard. *Black Boy*. New York: HarperPerennial, 1993.

Index